Brian Scovell is one of Dickie Bird's oldest associates. He began his journalistic career with the *Daily Sketch* in 1960 and joined the *Daily Mail* in 1971. He has written fifteen sports books, most of them about cricket, and was chairman of the Cricket Writers' Club from 1985–9. He is married to Audrey, an artist, and lives in Bromley, Kent.

DICKIE

A TRIBUTE TO UMPIRE HAROLD BIRD

edited by Brian Scovell

with specially commissioned cartoons
by Bill Tidy and Ken Mahood

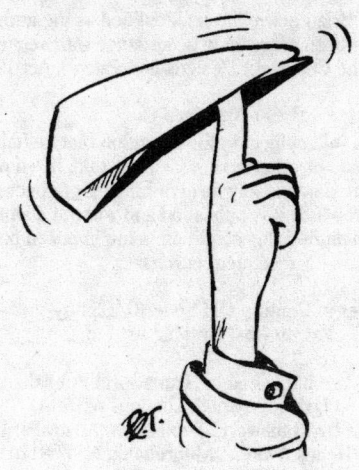

CORGI BOOKS

DICKIE
A CORGI BOOK : 0 552 14552 1

Originally published in Great Britain by Partridge Press,
a division of Transworld Publishers Ltd

PRINTING HISTORY
Partridge Press edition published 1996
Corgi edition published 1997

Set in Century Old Style 10/12pt by
Falcon Oast Graphic Art Ltd

Corgi Books are published by Transworld Publishers Ltd,
61–63 Uxbridge Road, London, W5 5SA,
in Australia by Transworld Publishers (Australia) Ltd,
15–25 Helles Avenue, Moorebank, NSW 2170
and in New Zealand by Transworld Publishers (NZ) Ltd,
3 William Pickering Drive, Albany, Auckland.

Reproduced, printed and bound in Great Britain by
Cox & Wyman Ltd, Reading, Berks.

ACKNOWLEDGEMENTS

It has been immense fun speaking to so many people in cricket about one of the game's greatest characters, Dickie Bird. He is a man who brings a smile to your face, a Jacques Tati of umpiring whose mannerisms have amused and delighted millions around the world.

When Dickie announced his retirement from international cricket at the end of January 1996, it left little time to contact everyone who might have had an anecdote or an opinion about him. I am grateful to David Graveney, the chief executive of the Professional Cricketers' Association, for helping me out by circulating his key members. Unfortunately, not too many of today's cricketers seem to respond to letters!

As usual, those who are the best known and the busiest were the first to oblige and I thank them all. Thanks also to David Welch, sports editor of *The Daily Telegraph*, Dominic Lawson, editor of the *Sunday Telegraph*, Michael Doggart of Collins Willow, Arthur Barker Ltd, the *Daily Mail* and the *Independent* for permission to use previously published material. Many thanks to Bill Tidy for the chapter motifs and to both Bill and Ken Mahood for the specially commissioned cartoons.

Last of all, sincere thanks to the man himself for his enthusiastic backing.

PICTURE CREDITS

Photographs supplied by Patrick Eagar except for: Adrian Murrell/Allsport colour p. 3 (both), p. 4 bottom, black & white p. 3 top, p. 8; Mike Hewitt/Allsport colour p. 2 left; Author black & white p. 2 top; Graham Chadwick/Empics colour p. 7 top; Joyner/Popperfoto colour p. 6 top left; Lawrence Griffiths/Empics colour p. 7 bottom; Hulton Deutsch Collection/Allsport black & white p. 2 bottom; John Ireland/Lennard Associates, from *Cricket Characters* published by Stanley Paul, 1984 colour p. 8.

CONTENTS

10 DOWNING STREET
LONDON SW1A 2AA

THE PRIME MINISTER

Dickie Bird is in the line of Great British umpires which began with Frank Chester. Dickie was a one off – the consummate professional with unerringly accurate judgement, trusted by the players and loved by the spectators. On the pitch his delightful originality gave as much pleasure as the elegant cover drive. When Dickie was umpiring the game was never dull. Test match lovers the world over will miss him.

John Major

February 1996

DICKIE

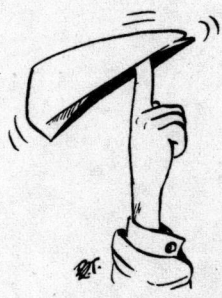

INTRODUCTION

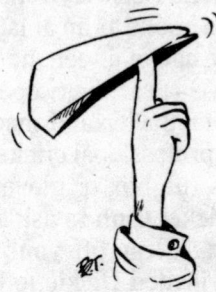

Brian Scovell

Dickie Bird, instantly recognized throughout the English-speaking world for his eccentricities, his extravagant gestures and his white cap, is one of the most loved and respected characters in world cricket. The stories about him are part of cricket's folklore.

Dickie ended his international career in June 1996 at Lord's with his 66th Test, a world record. 'I always said I wanted to go out at the top and I have,' he said proudly. He has many fond memories of Lord's where in 1973, when the Test against the West Indies was interrupted by a bomb scare, he refused to leave the middle. 'Safest place to be,' he said.

Few people are universally known by their first names, or in this case, a nickname, but he is. Christened Harold Dennis after his father James Harold who was a miner for fifty-two years, Dickie didn't really like his nickname but it has stuck with him and is a sign of the affection he generates, not just among cricket lovers but ordinary people.

All his childhood friends who played with him on a rough piece of ground near his home in Barnsley had nicknames. They played football in the winter and cricket in the summer and most of them had a common ambition: to play both sports for their country like their idol Willie Watson. One friend was Tommy Taylor, nicknamed 'Tucker', who went on to play for Manchester United and England and died in the Munich air crash in 1958.

Dickie played in the same Barnsley schools' side as Taylor and was on Barnsley FC's books as an amateur. But appearing for Barnsley YMCA at the age of fifteen, he damaged a knee in a tackle and had to have a cartilage operation. It virtually finished his career as a footballer and made him even more determined to become a professional cricketer. He packed his boots, shirt and trousers (no box or gloves) in a carrier bag and went to Barnsley Cricket Club to ask for a trial. The first person he met told him, 'Clear off you!' But another club member, Alf Broadhead, invited Dickie to bowl in the nets to him. Though Dickie was an unpretentious medium pacer, Barnsley signed him. He became an opening batsman, a nudger and a pusher. One of his partners early on in his career was a reporter on the *South Yorkshire Times*, Michael Parkinson.

Barnsley paid him £4 a week, which wasn't enough to live on and he followed his father into coal mining as a fitter. He declined to go underground: 'I wouldn't do that if they paid me £135 a week,' he said. When he was recommended to Yorkshire for a trial the pit manager refused to let him have the necessary day off. The manager ran the colliery cricket team and knowing that as a professional Dickie wasn't eligible to play in the National Coal Board knock-out competition told him he would relent if he played for him under an assumed name. Dickie agreed and played under the name of George Copping.

Dickie went by bus to Headingley for his trial. Almost half a century later, he can remember every ball bowled to him. The bowlers were Bob Appleyard, one of the finest exponents of the off cutter in the game's history, Johnny Wardle, one of the greatest slow left-arm bowlers this country has ever produced and an eighteen-year-old fast bowler who was aiming to impress by the name of Fred Trueman. 'I had fifteen minutes in the net and didn't lay bat on ball,' he said. Arthur Mitchell, the coach, told him not to bother to come back. But Maurice Leyland, the other coach, was more compassionate and after a few more less taxing net sessions Dickie was taken on to the staff in 1952 at a salary of £12.50 a week.

Five years later, at the age of twenty-four, he finally made the first team. There was immense competition for places. One of his rivals, though seven years younger, was Geoffrey Boycott.

Two years later he recorded his highest score of 181 in seven and a half hours against Glamorgan at Bradford only to be told by chairman Brian Sellers: 'Well played, but get thee head down, Dickie lad, you're in the second team next match.' Realizing he would never make the grade in the tough Yorkshire school, he signed for Leicestershire – 'the biggest mistake of my career' as he later recalled.

In 1965 he left Grace Road, totally disillusioned, and began coaching at Plymouth College, a public school, and played as a professional for Paignton. He took the MCC's Advanced Coaching Certificate, part of which was a paper on the laws of the game, and was successful enough to apply to Lord's to join the first-class umpires' panel. Unlike footballers, cricketers can retire from playing and go straight into umpiring and Dickie's application was accepted at the start of the 1970 season.

He was so nervous the day he made his début that he woke up in the middle of the night and was outside the Oval at 6.30 a.m. The match was Surrey *v* Yorkshire and his fellow umpire was the crotchety Australian, Cec Pepper. The ground was locked up and he tried to climb over a wall. A passing policeman spotted him. 'I'm one of the umpires,' he explained. 'Go on,' said the constable, 'you'll be telling me next you are the Prime Minister.' The game was ruined by rain and bad light.

'I wanted to get the game going but Cec kept saying "you suggest nothing, you just sit there," ' he recalled. At the end of the season the MCC secretary, Billy Griffith, sent him a letter of congratulation. The longest, most successful and most entertaining umpiring career had begun. He was later to explain his phobia about light. 'I was standing in a Test in 1976 when Viv Richards drove the ball straight down the pitch and I didn't see it,' he said. 'I could have been killed. I've seen batsmen hit the ball at fielders and they've been hurt. You can't take the risk.'

The elements have played a conspicuous part in his career. At Buxton in 1975 he was forced to abandon play in a county game because of snow and in 1988 there was the mystery of water seeping under the surrounds at Headingley. At Old Trafford in 1995 he made the national news again when he stopped play because of the sun reflecting in the players' eyes. As he came off to remonstrate with supporters, one said, 'Calm down Dickie old son, come and have a drink.'

Dickie was the other umpire when Arthur Fagg, upset by a show of dissent by West Indies skipper Rohan Kanhai at Edgbaston in 1973, refused to continue in the match. Dickie has never been in that confrontational situation himself because he has the ability to calm tempers with a light-hearted remark followed by a friendly warning.

He umpired his first Test at Headingley in 1973 where Boycott made a century against New Zealand and four years later he stood in the Test at Trent Bridge when Boycott recorded yet another 100. Dickie received a warmer welcome than usual in that match because it had just been announced he had turned down an offer to join Kerry Packer's circus.

He also rejected an offer to umpire in South Africa when the South Africans were banned from world cricket. He has always said, 'I am not in it for the money. I love the game and would never do anything to harm it.' When the ICC set up their international panel of umpires in 1992 Dickie was one of the first umpires to be named on it. He has officiated in every Test-match-playing country except South Africa and earned the respect of all the players.

For some years a number of them, headed by former England captain Mike Gatting, jokingly referred to him as a 'not outer'. But he always maintains, 'I would rather be sure than sorry. They didn't call me that when I gave six lbws in the West Indies *v* Pakistan Test in 1993 when Steve Bucknor and I gave seventeen between us, a world record.' The arrival of the television monitor and the third umpire has made it much harder for the officials and Dickie, a reluctant convert to the idea of off-field assistance, believes technology has to be kept in check.

Dickie lives a bachelor existence in a seventeenth-century cottage at Staincross, on the outskirts of Barnsley. Geoff Boycott lives a few miles away at Woolley, but they rarely see each other. The founder of the Methodists, John Wesley, once slept in an upstairs bedroom at the cottage. Marjorie, his sister who is married to a stonemason, comes in regularly to do his cleaning, and the garden, which stretches at the back to a stone wall, is maintained by a gardener who pops in occasionally.

The two rooms downstairs are full of framed pictures, cups, trophies and other souvenirs of his life in cricket. Letters from Buckingham Palace inviting him to have lunch with the Queen are framed and have pride of place. The first one that arrived in 1977 is addressed to 'Mr and Mrs Dickie Bird'. The error was soon put right. His spacious desk is covered with letters from all around the world and he answers every one, by hand.

There is little sign of ostentation about his house or his possessions, but as everyone knows when he is away, and the house has been burgled on several occasions, steel bars and shutters protect the windows and doors.

His decision to retire after his 66th Test was seen by everyone in the game as an eminently sensible one because it meant he quit while at the top of his profession – to a fanfare of trumpets.

1

'... GET THEE HEAD DOWN, DICKIE LAD, YOU'RE IN SECOND TEAM NEXT MATCH'

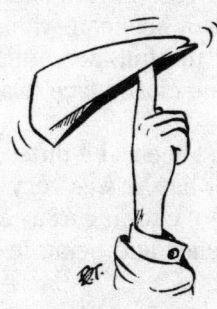

Dickie never quite made it as a cricketer. His career average in 170 innings for Yorkshire and Leicestershire was 20.71, and he made fourteen appearances in Yorkshire's first team (1956–59) and seventy-nine for Leicestershire for whom he played between 1960 and 1964.

The nadir of his career came, ironically, moments after he made the highest score of his career, 181 not out against Glamorgan at Bradford in 1959. As he came into the dressing room, Brian Sellers, the Yorkshire chairman, said to him, '... get thee head down, Dickie lad, you're in the second team next match.'

He was, too, and it broke his heart. He played just two more matches at the end of that season. His final innings for Yorkshire was 'bowled Harold Rhodes 0'. At the start of the next season he scored 89 in a practice match and, told that he was still in the second team, broke down and went home to write for his release. He joined Leicestershire, only to find the captain Maurice Hallam was not too well disposed towards Yorkshiremen!

Ray Illingworth
Former England and Yorkshire captain

The ex-BBC analyst and chairman of selectors goes back a long way with Dickie.

I played with Dickie at Yorkshire but not very often because he only played when the Test players were away on Test duty. But I remember him as a batsman who played with a very straight bat. He gave it the full face, unlike some of today's players who play with the closed face, playing the ball to the legside.

If his temperament had been a bit different I think he would have made a career of it but he was very nervous. Before he went in, he would sit there chewing away at his batting gloves. He was short of confidence and being in and out of the side didn't help.

He admits he made a mistake going to play for Leicestershire and I think he was right. Leicestershire were a bit of an undisciplined lot in those days. They had a few players who liked a drink. Dickie was never one of them. Half a pint was as much as he managed.

I must say I was surprised when he took up umpiring. I thought his nerves would let him down like they had some others. But he handled things really well. He has never been afraid to sort things out in the middle and he has always done it in such a way, with a smile on his face, that he commands the respect of all the players. There is not one who doesn't like him as a person.

He has kept himself fit and lasted a long time in a job which has a lot of pressure. It's life and death to him.

My last Test as England captain was the famous bomb scare Test at Lord's in 1973 at the height of the IRA bombing campaign. The police ordered the ground to be cleared at two forty and the West Indies players went back to their hotel. Dickie sat out in the middle on the covers. He said it was the safest place to be. I spent my time in the car park with police who were examining cars to see if the bomb was under one of them. I thought to myself, 'I'm a silly bugger doing this. I should be out in the middle with Dickie.'

I think he is retiring at just the right time. When you get older it is easier to make mistakes and when you've been as good as he's been you don't want people to go around saying you're past it. He's doing it the right way, going out with his head held high. He's not bitter and twisted about it.

He'll always make a living. He's a good public speaker which again shows his character because that really can make you nervous. He's overcome that as he's overcome everything else. And he's got a few bob put away. Good luck to him. He's been a great servant to the game.

Don Shepherd
Former Glamorgan bowler

The former offspin bowler, now a journalist, was on the receiving end when Dickie made his highest score.

A typical after-dinner speech by Dickie will always make reference to his career best 181 not out when opening the batting for Yorkshire against Glamorgan at Bradford in May 1959. His next line will be, 'And do you know, I were then dropped for the next game!'

He was replaced by first-team regular Ken Taylor who two weeks later opened for England against India at Trent Bridge. Described by *Wisden* as a twenty-six-year-old Colt – one of five uncapped players in the side – Dickie batted for seven and a half hours on a pitch which although easing out on the second day had been juicy enough for the great FS to take 5–56 in our first innings and was never docile.

I have to say this, Glamorgan's usually efficient fielding was not up to its usual standard and Dickie was dropped at 53 and 102. We blamed the difficult backgrounds! But to his credit Dickie battled on and contributed almost half his side's runs in their 405–8, enabling them to win by an innings and 35 runs. We had a reasonable side that year, finishing sixth in the championship.

As one of the sufferers – I bowled forty-two overs – I congratulated Dickie on his innings. If he hadn't scored it and we had held our catches, what would he have to speak about at these dinners?

Furthermore, the Yorkshire selection policy of the time probably helped propel him along the road which led to fame as a Test match umpire of the highest calibre who enjoys worldwide respect.

Doug Insole

Former Essex and England batsman and leading
cricket administrator

———

*Doug Insole describes the time Dickie fell to Essex leg spinner Bill
Greensmith after Brian Close was indiscreet.*

It gives me no pleasure to confess that in 1959 I was at least
partially responsible for Dickie's demise as a Yorkshire
cricketer, although I comfort myself with the knowledge that
the man chiefly responsible was Brian Close.

It was in mid-July at Scarborough where the Yorkshire
committee had assembled to decide on which of its players
should be retained for the following season. Closey was the
not-out batsman standing at the Trafalgar Square End, away
from the pavilion, when Dickie, a fragile figure, prepared to
take guard. 'Good luck, Dickie, lad,' said Brian. 'They'll all be
watching you. And don't worry, I'll take the leg spinner.'

Never having seen Dickie bat before, I was completely
unaware of his alleged vulnerability against leg spin until
apprised of the fact by Closey, who was presumably trying to
be helpful to his junior partner. 'You might have a job, Brian,'
I said to Closey, 'we've got two leggies, so you're going to have
to play every ball!' We had indeed got two leg spinners, Bill
Greensmith, a useful home-grown performer, and the late
Bertie Clarke, who had played for the West Indies and was
specially registered by us because we were short of finger
spinners.

Already in a state, having been reminded by his partner of
the significance of the occasion, Dickie proved Closey's diag-
nosis to be correct and he succumbed twice in the match to
leg spin, making a dodgy ten runs in the process. Bill
Greensmith got him both times. I think he only played one
more match for Yorkshire after that.

Sorry about that, Dickie, but it was all, as I subsequently
realized, part of a deeply laid plot to accelerate your début as
an umpire! I was chairman of the Umpires' Committee when

Harold Dennis Bird first stood in a Test match and like most other people I was aware that we had found somebody a bit special.

There came a time, however, when our hero seemed to me and to some others, to have become somewhat over demonstrative in his signalling and in his general control of the game. So one Saturday morning at Lord's I asked him to come in for a chat. The gist of my message was that although there was no wish to stifle his very personal approach to umpiring he should perhaps remember that the crowd's priority was almost certainly to watch the cricket rather than the umpiring. I knew him well enough to say it and his response was immediate and highly satisfactory. 'I know what you mean, sir, and I thank you for telling me,' he said. He was, even then, good news.

He talked to me subsequently about the extremely remunerative approach he had had from Kerry Packer and later still, from South Africa and, as is well known, he decided to remain completely loyal to the established game, which will, I am certain, wish to retain his services in an ambassadorial and tutorial role after his retirement from Test cricket. He is, in my opinion, the genuine article.

Mike Turner
The former Leicestershire secretary and chief executive

_____

The man who brought Dickie to Grace Road in 1965.

Dickie had a lot of ability as a batsman but never did his talents justice because he was so jittery. He had one or two big scores, but in seventy-nine matches he scored 2,107 runs for an average of 19 which wasn't really enough to keep him on the staff.

Leicestershire hadn't won anything since their formation in 1879 and there were times when we propped up the table. Our successes were to come later. But we did have a number of sound players who I thought had the makings of umpires, including Chris Balderstone, Barry Dudleston, Jack Birkenshaw and Ray Julian. There was also Dickie, despite his nervousness.

I told him he ought to take up umpiring and recommended him to Lord's. I felt someone as conscientious and true as he was, someone who really cared about cricket, would do a very good job and I was delighted to be proved right. Dickie told everyone, 'It's the best thing next to playing and it will keep me in the first-class game.'

That was in June 1969 and he tells the story of how he went to see his father who was in hospital to tell him the news. The next day his father died and it was one of Dickie's biggest regrets that he never saw him umpire a first-class match.

Maurice Hallam
Former Leicestershire opening batsman and captain

Maurice was Dickie's captain at Leicestershire and he denies he had a down on Yorkshiremen!

Dickie was one of the most tense cricketers I ever played with and sometimes we had a job getting him out of the dressing room to open the innings. It's amazing really that he took up umpiring and was such a marvellous success at it.

He never really produced the figures to have a long career as a player. His average when he was with us was less than twenty. In his first book he blamed me for his being sacked but the committee approved the decision and I think that now he will admit it was the right decision. It turned out to be the making of him because he went into umpiring and his career just took off.

He was always a 100 per cent team man. When you were batting with him he would keep up a stream of encouraging remarks. 'Good shot,' he'd say. 'Keep it going, you're doing great.' And things like that.

On 30 July 1960 we set a county record in a game against the touring South Africans of 277. I made 164 and he made 107. But I must say the bowlers weren't the most demanding. Geoff Griffin had been no-balled at Lord's by Syd Buller and was playing as a batsman.

A wine company put up a crate of sherry for any batsman who scored a century and Dickie and I each won twenty-four bottles. 'What are we going to do with it, skipper?' he asked. 'Well Dickie,' I said, 'there are nine others in the side who might like a bottle.'

In his book he said I had a down on Yorkshiremen but that wasn't true. I used to say, 'If you are going to beat Yorkshiremen, you've got to play like them and give them nothing.' That's what we tried to do. Yorkshiremen stick together.

Dickie recalls that he was injured in one match at Worcester when he crashed into Jack Birkenshaw and hurt a shoulder going for a high catch. As the ball went into the air I called 'Dickie' and Stanley Jayasinghe called 'Jack'.

I saw Dickie recently at Grace Road and he was sitting in the umpires' room in an interval. 'The bell's gone,' I said jokingly. 'Time to get out there.' He jumped up. 'Don't give me any more hassle, I've got enough problems,' he said.

Jack van Geloven
Former Yorkshire and Leicestershire all-rounder

Now a coach at a school in Edinburgh. His career closely followed Dickie's ... except he was a much better cricketer.

Dickie and I were friends from our early days as schoolboy cricketers and footballers. He was a good footballer, was Dickie. He could have made the grade but for injury. I played against him a lot and I had a lot of respect for him.

We played together for the Yorkshire Second team and then at Leicestershire and we had four years rooming together in a pub next to Grace Road. When I got married and lived in a house near the ground he would come round for Sunday lunch. He would always insist on Yorkshire pudding.

I think he got too much wrapped up in the game. If he had got married and had a family I think it would have changed him. He did have a girlfriend once when we played at Leicestershire and he was close to an engagement. But it didn't happen. As he says now, he got married to cricket!

I remember one day we were playing a county game at Grace Road and for some reason he was under the impression we were batting first although Willie Watson, the captain, hadn't tossed. Off went Willie to the middle with the opposing captain and Dickie proceeded to put his pads on.

He was so jittery that he started putting the left one on his right leg and when he'd done that, he strapped the other one on his left leg. The rest of the players were watching from the other side of the dressing room and were in stitches.

Willie came back and said, 'What are you up to? We're in the field.' Dickie said, 'Thank God for that!'

I had a few years on the umpires' list and remember one occasion when Yorkshire, captained by Geoffrey Boycott, were playing Gloucestershire, captained by Mike Procter, at Scarborough where I live and the first day was washed out. There was heavy rain all night and when I arrived next morn-

28

ing Dickie said, 'It's fit to start at 11 a.m. The groundsman has just told me.'

'Are you sure?' I said. 'It's under water out there. We'll not start before lunch.'

'Oh my God,' said Dickie. 'Where's Joe Lister [the secretary]? We've got to stop them coming in. I've said it will be a prompt start.'

It was a gloriously sunny day and within a short space of time ten thousand people had come into the ground. And they were expecting some action. Dickie daren't go out of the umpires' room. We sat there waiting for the square to dry out. Dickie was in a state. It was four thirty-five before play began!

There was another story I like about Dickie, when he was standing in a Test at Headingley and the teams had come off several times for rain and bad light. Every time he went out to inspect the conditions he found himself in a spat with spectators. I was there visiting and thought I would have some fun. I told him I had heard some yobs had tried to set fire to a car in the car park and described the vehicle which bore a close resemblance to his own. Dickie really thought it was his car and began flapping about!

Jim Parks

Former Sussex and England wicket-keeper/batsman

The popular former wicket-keeper/batsman recalls an embarrassing moment for Dickie.

Dickie will not appreciate me mentioning this but I believe he goes into the record books as being the batsman who recorded the quickest ever king pair!

It happened when he was opening the batting for Leicestershire and the match was Leicestershire *v* Sussex at Grace Road in August 1960. The game was played in very humid conditions and I have never seen the ball swing so much. Sussex won the toss and Ted Dexter, who was captain, decided to bat first. We struggled to 239 with last man, Robin Marlar, making 39.

Dickie opened with Willie Watson, the former England opener and ex-soccer international and was out first ball, caught by Alan Oakman off the bowling of Ian Thomson. Leicestershire were bowled out for 42 in twenty-four overs and were made to follow on. Not much time remained when Dickie, looking more nervous than ever, came out with Willie for the start of the second innings. Ian, who was not the worst performer when the ball was swinging, ran in and again bowled an unplayable ball. Dickie got a nick and was caught by Hubert Doggart for another first ball duck.

It was about the only time I can remember him speechless ... but only for a second or two!

Dickie tells the story himself of how I became the first batsman he gave out and then recalled. It was in his second year on the list and the game was Sussex *v* Middlesex at Hove. John Price was bowling to Peter Graves and Peter drove the ball straight back at him. John got a touch and the ball hit the stumps. In the split second that followed, I left my ground and after an appeal, Dickie gave me out. But I knew that at the moment the bails came off, I was still in the crease. I didn't say anything but as I walked off towards the pavilion Dickie went

to Mike Brearley, the Middlesex captain and said, 'I am sorry
but I am going to call him back. I made a mistake.' Brearley
said, 'You're correct.'

Brian Statham
Former Lancashire and England bowler

One of English cricket's greatest bowlers, Brian always liked bowling to Dickie!

I played in that match in 1960 when Leicestershire were bowled out for 37, their lowest total since the Second World War. Dickie retired hurt after scoring 1 in the first innings. It was a flier of a pitch and the ball caught him on the knuckle. He was in agony and didn't come out for the second innings.

I see in *Wisden* he played in the next match against Hampshire and bagged a pair. I bet he wished he hadn't! I don't think he scored too many against me. That's a naughty thing to say but it is true. He's a great lad.

We played together in the first Gillette Cup tie played in this country, Lancashire *v* Leicestershire at Old Trafford in May 1963, and I think I got him cheaply then too. He used to edge me through the slips but it didn't concern me. 'Don't worry,' I would say, 'that's another four runs for you!' He always thanked me.

Ray Lewis
Former FIFA referee

The former referee talks about how his catch stopped Dickie picking up a £2 bonus.

I've met Dickie on numerous occasions and have always found him a friendly guy, much respected by everyone. He would attend matches at Bramall Lane when I refereed there and we'd have a chat for ten or fifteen minutes.

I used to remind him that I got him out once when he played for Paignton. My club Mill Hill Park toured Devon and we usually played at Paignton. Dickie was the professional there and used to be paid a bonus of £5 for a hundred and £2 for a fifty. That meant he was a difficult man to get out! He was similar to Trevor Bailey in style, or even Geoff Boycott. In this particular match he had been in almost a couple of hours and was approaching his fifty when he nicked one and I caught it behind the stumps. He walked – he was very genuine then and still is.

As an umpire he's a man who will always call the tight ones, the decisions that can change a game. I am not too familiar with all the cricketing laws but I believe he applies them rigidly, and is not afraid to do so. But he does it with a smile and a joke.

I would compare him to the likes of Kevin Howley, Jack Taylor, Arthur Holland and a few other referees of twenty or more years ago – characters who spoke a lot to the players and commanded their respect. You don't see that kind of referee today because the game has changed. It is so much faster and FIFA and UEFA have brought down the age limits so that officials are younger and less experienced. If someone had to name the seven referees from this country on the FIFA list he wouldn't be able to do it. He would a few years ago.

If Dickie was a football referee I don't think he would be able to control matches the way he does in cricket. You have to be younger and fitter to cope with all the new demands.

I believe Dickie still has a lot to offer when he finally retires from the first-class game. They should use his experience as a third umpire, or ICC referee and he will be invaluable as a lecturer.

Clive Radley

MCC head coach and former England and Middlesex batsman

Clive Radley delighted in Dickie's company when they coached together in South Africa.

I had eight years out in South Africa with Dickie between 1966 and 1975 coaching in Johannesburg. There were four of us; Mike and Derek Taylor, the twins who played for Hampshire and Somerset, shared one car and Dickie and I the other. We stayed in this massive 900-room hotel in Hillbrow which in those days was a very lively area, full of clubs and pubs. I was out there recently and it had changed a lot. It's become almost a no-go area for whites.

Everyone knew Dickie. He quickly became a celebrity with his constant chat and peculiar mannerisms. He would sit on the huge settee in the lounge at the hotel rummaging around after coins which slipped out of his pocket down the back of the cushions. He eventually used a handkerchief to tie up his loose change and we used to make jokes about it.

We went out there on one trip on a liner from Southampton and Dickie got in a state before we boarded the ship. 'Get me a doctor,' he said. 'I don't feel well.' I have to explain that he was a bit of a hypochondriac. The doctor gave him an injection for seasickness and he was confined to his cabin for the first two days while we sunbathed on deck and had a good time. On one trip we spent a night in a small shack-type place in Kruger Park. Lions and hyenas were making a tremendous noise and Dickie was panicking. It was also extremely hot and he woke us up in the night shouting, 'I'm dying. It's too hot!' He was splashing water all over himself. He managed to survive!

On one trip he showed us a letter from Lord's offering him a job on the umpires' list. 'What shall I do?' he kept asking. 'Do you think I should take it? What would you do?' We advised him to have a go and it was the best thing he ever did.

When I played for Middlesex and he was umpiring he gave me out on the front foot a few times. Not many batsmen can

35

claim that! He used to give me out down at Hove when Mike 'Mini' Buss hit me on the pad. Mini bowled slow, swingey stuff, left arm over the wicket, and he would appeal and Dickie would raise the finger. But he didn't give many out on the front foot. I was one of the unlucky ones.

Mike Taylor
Former Hampshire and Nottinghamshire bowler

With his twin brother Derek, Mike was another of the English coaches who worked with Dickie in South Africa. Dickie gave up going to South Africa once the Gleneagles Agreement ruled against sporting links with South Africa.

Dickie was terrified of flying and when we went out there on the first trip he worked himself up into a terrible state. The flight seemed endless, with no less than three stops between London and Johannesburg. Every now and again Dickie would ask me to look out the window and would say: 'Can you see owt, lad?' As we were 30,000 feet above the South Atlantic at the time it was a rather futile question.

Working for the Transvaal Cricket Union as coaches, we had to share transport, an old Ford Anglia. 'I'll have to drive because if I sit in the passenger's seat I'll be sick,' he said. That was before I had been given the chance to drive, so he had to take the wheel. A bit of an old woman! To make matters worse he had to have the car for three and a half days per week regardless!

The hotel chef was a Zulu chief and how he translated 'Are you alreet, t'old lad?' spoken in a broad Barnsley accent remains a mystery to this day.

Television had yet to be introduced to South Africa and as a result self-entertainment was high on the agenda. Dickie's rendering of the various songs from the 'Black and White Minstrel Show' accompanied by Phil Sharpe and Don Wilson took over many parties to the delight of our South African hosts. By sheer coincidence, a version of the 'Black and White Minstrel Show' was touring South Africa under the politically convenient name of the 'Minstrel Scandals' which provided a timely, lyrical refresher for the Yorkshire songsters.

However, my abiding memory of Dickie is seeing him at the Wanderers Club swimming pool – surrounded by wealth and opulence – with his white handkerchief knotted at four corners perched on his head to combat the African sun, epitomizing a Yorkshireman abroad!

Some years later, after establishing himself as one of the leading umpires in the world, the High School at which he coached in Johannesburg did not allow him to umpire their matches. Having recently witnessed the remarkable standard of umpiring achieved by South Africa during the winter of 1996 I suppose you can understand the reasoning!

Kevin Lyons
First-class umpire and county coach

––––––––––

Kevin, who also coached with Dickie in South Africa, recounts the story of how Dickie lost his shirt in Johannesburg.

Dickie was head coach at the Transvaal Cricket Union when I went to Johannesburg in the late Sixties and I remember the day he received a letter from Lord's saying he had been appointed on the first-class umpires' list. 'I'm on,' he shouted. 'They've taken me on!' He promised he would treat us all to champagne when he got back to London. Thirty years on, we are still waiting.

He was always particular about what he wore and took pride in looking after his clothes. A maid used to wash our clothes for us and one day he came in and said his best yellow shirt was missing. No-one could find it but a day or two later Dickie was walking down the street when he saw the maid's boyfriend wearing it. He went bananas, shouting and gesticulating in the street. People couldn't fathom what was going on. I can't remember if he got it back.

I have been the third umpire at Test matches when he has stood in matches and I always marvelled at the way his demeanour changed once he was about to go out to the middle. In the hours before the start of play he would be like a caged tiger. Or a boxer waiting for a big fight.

The five-minute bell would go and he quickly became a different personality. It was like a batsman who knew he was good at something. He had the confidence to do it although he was basically a nervous and insular person. And he always got on so well with the players, defusing any situation with a few words and a laugh or two. He enjoyed it and those qualities – laughter, enjoying it and making people laugh – are dying in sport, aren't they? It's sad really.

2

THE CAPTAINS GIVE DICKIE THEIR MARKS

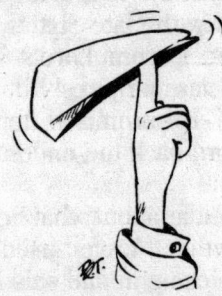

Umpires stand or fall by the marks they are given by captains. And ever since he became an umpire, Dickie has received high marks, particularly from the captains of the international teams.

Sir Colin Cowdrey
Former England and Kent captain

———

Colin Cowdrey was knighted not only for his feats on the cricket field but also for his contribution as an administrator and as chairman of ICC he helped bring in the independent panel of Test umpires.

I am not surprised there has been a hose-pipe ban in Yorkshire now for some years. It stems from that Test match at Headingley in 1988 when a water-pipe burst just off the square and Dickie was the umpire! I was present in my capacity as chairman of ICC and though it seemed funny to us at the time I am sure it caused heartache to Dickie because it meant he had to endure the wrath of the crowd.

It wasn't his fault, of course, but he took it in typically good humour. It is no coincidence that he has been involved in some of the major and unusual incidents at Test matches in recent times. It seems a role he has been destined to fill for many of his years as a leading umpire.

I was weaned on two umpires of the old school, Frank Chester and Alec Skelding, both somewhat autocratic characters, eccentrics in their way. They had a disciplined training as young cricketers and were products of an age which learned to accept authority and as a result were ready to wield it aright. Chester was precise and pernickety but of the highest class. Skelding had the players on his side, for he could be relied on to bring humour to brighten the dullest day and was given to occasional outbursts of verse.

It is not essential but it helps to have played the game at the highest level. The advent of sponsorship and the hurly-burly of limited-overs cricket brought a new, more combative element into the game and has made a new range of demands on umpires. Accepted, old-fashioned codes have been eroded as winning became so much more important and, unhappily, umpires could no longer look to the captain when players went too far.

In this more challenging environment, Dickie Bird emerged to become one of the most respected and best-loved personalities of his day. He has so many attributes I have mentioned and more. Lucky to have been a good player himself, he has something of Chester's efficiency, Skelding's sense of fun, Frank Lee's sensitivity, Syd Buller's courage and calm, the clever touch of Dusty Rhodes, the dignity and bonhomie of John Langridge, Arthur Fagg's perception of the game and Charlie Elliott's interest in the welfare of the players.

Highly strung, given to mannerisms and conscientious in the extreme, Dickie had more than sufficient strength to cope with the turbulent and highly competitive attitudes of the modern game. He was able to be firm without being officious, uncompromising in executing the law, yet intensely human and ready to smile. I hope he will continue to remain in the forefront of the game in some capacity.

David Gower
Former England and Leicestershire captain
and television commentator

Dickie umpired David's first Test, against Pakistan in 1978 and also his hundredth, against the West Indies.

Harold Dennis, Dickie to his chums, Bird is a magnet for tales of the unexpected. Curiously enough, it is probably because of the respect which he commands from the world's top players, allied to his naturally quirky and immensely good-natured character, that some of those same players have at times treated him with scant evidence of that respect.

Allan Lamb and Ian Botham are normally fundamental to most of the stories associated with Dickie, mobile phones ringing in his pocket, flaming newspapers thrust under the door of the umpires' room, the door of course locked, and on one occasion Lambie even commandeered an Indian soldier, supposedly on security duties in the team's Delhi hotel, and sent him into Dickie's hotel room, where the world's most famous umpire was quietly suffering from some dreadful lurgy. Such an awakening, with a rifle muzzle nudging his nose, was not quite what the doctor ordered!

As an umpire, Dickie has somehow kept his head above water for what seems an awfully long time, in an era when umpires have been subjected to unprecedented pressures, especially from the dreaded television-replay syndrome. Never have umpires' mistakes been so closely analysed as in the last ten years, and many a good man has begun well only to wilt under the pressure.

By and large players will cope with the odd rough decision, and more easily so if they have respect for the umpire concerned, and any umpire who has the ability to get on with players and shows the right sort of friendly but commanding attitude out on the field will find the resulting atmosphere a better one in which to work, a principle which applies to umpires anywhere in the world.

Dickie certainly achieved such command, and still retains it, but he also retains all those foibles that have helped create the legend, including his own special form of aquaphobia: basically if there is any moisture in the atmosphere, or even just the bad light brought on by the clouds that bring the moisture, Dickie is a nervous wreck.

How fitting then, that during the Headingley Test of 1988 against the West Indies, as it happens my hundredth for England, Dickie should be standing at the Football Stand End when, of all things, an underground pipe burst slap bang in the middle of Curtly Ambrose's run up. There wasn't a cloud in the sky to worry about, so when the West Indies' main strike force, all six foot eight of him, looked down at Dickie with that bright blue sky framing his glowering features and announced there was a flood gushing up from what should have been bone-dry turf, Dickie would have realized immediately that it wasn't going to be an easy day.

Hands on hips, flat cap pushed back on his head, he muttered his way to the edge of the field – 'It's not my fault, it's not my fault' – and summoned the ground staff to sort out the problem. And in due course all was indeed sorted, with plenty of time to spare later in the afternoon for Dickie to yet again raise the finger to signify the end of a very short Gower cameo, once more in the book 'caught Dujon'.

Make no bones about it though, Dickie's career has been based solidly on a genuine talent for the task of umpiring, and the events that led to the many stories that have been accumulated around him would never have happened but for his continuing skill in the execution of his duties. Also nobody transmits a love for the game as surely as Harold Dennis Bird, and I for one will miss his presence in the Test match arena, a stage which has brought him a reputation unsurpassed in his field.

Geoff Boycott
Former Yorkshire and England opening batsman
and television commentator

Dickie's close neighbour gives his expert verdict on his former batting partner.

I used to play in the Yorkshire League with Dickie at Barnsley and even then he was renowned for the nervous twitching gestures which delight or infuriate so many people today. Sometimes he was so nervous before going in to bat I had to put his gloves on for him.

When he took up umpiring many people were afraid he would not stand the pressure but he has bridged the gap with amazing success. He is definitely England's top umpire – and that is not just my opinion. It is borne out by his marks from county captains' reports during the season and by the number of Tests in which he has been asked to stand.

His mannerisms are famous – or notorious. Stooping over the wickets like a vulture, short coat tucked up beneath his arms, peering from beneath a penguin cap with arms flicking, wrists twirling. A bundle of nervous energy. But the players respect him because they know he is always in charge, concentrating on every delivery. He will have a chat with players he knows and can throw back a cutting reply with the best of them if he is challenged, while remaining firm and authoritative, friendly but not familiar.

He is very positive, always determined to get on with the game as quickly as possible, ready to gallop to the pavilion to sort matters out if necessary – and that cannot be bad from the spectators' point of view. Yet he is never hasty when making a decision: he will give himself a second or two to collect his thoughts and weigh the pros and cons. Players appreciate that approach more than an umpire, right or wrong, who fires off an instant decision.

Off the field he is great company, a wonderful teller of tales punctuated with all the old familiar gestures. That is the point about Dickie – he is entirely natural. His gestures come as readily to him now as they did twenty-seven years ago when I first saw him umpiring and he was a long, long way from being a Test umpire. Those who suggest it is affectation do not know the man. If you asked Dickie Bird to cut out all his mannerisms, to slow down and stop getting into the action quite so often he really would not know what you were talking about.

In the Centenary Test in 1980 the match turned out to be an anti-climax because of the weather and England never got into a position to win. I followed the instructions of the captain, Ian Botham, in making sure we didn't lose by scoring an unbeaten 128, frustrating the Australians in the process. Len Pascoe reacted by frequently pitching short. I was so wrapped up in my innings that I did not really appreciate Dickie's intervention but it took the following course:

Dickie: 'That's enough Lennie. Keep the ball a bit further up.'
Lennie: 'I don't know what you mean. I'm not bowling short.'
Dickie: 'You are, and I'm telling you to stop.'
Greg Chappell: (Australian captain) 'He's not bowling too short.'
Dickie: 'I have made my decision and I'm not asking for other opinions.'

With that he marched off to inform his colleague David Constant of the first warning, making it quite clear that the argument was over. Finally, Lennie conceded: 'All right, Dickie. You're the boss.'

A weaker umpire than Dickie might have easily backed away from possible confrontation but that is not his style and he is respected throughout the world for invariably being both fair and firm.

Adapted with permission from Boycott: The Autobiography *(Partridge Press) and* Opening Up *(Arthur Barker) by Geoffrey Boycott.*

Brian Close
Former Yorkshire and England captain

———

Dickie's former Yorkshire team-mate recalls how he gave him advice, which was taken.

There will only be one Dickie Bird. He is unique and there will never be anyone like him. Lovable, excitable, passionately in love with the game ... everything was almost like an orgasm for him.

As a player, he needed understanding and encouraging. As an umpire he needed reassurance but he was a great umpire, there's no doubt about that. His actions and mannerisms made him the character he was, not so much what he said. He was so funny and cricket is about humour.

I saw him last season and I said to him, 'You want to make sure you get out while you're still at the top Dickie, old lad.' I'm glad he's taken my advice. He will always be welcomed wherever cricket is played throughout the world.

M. J. K. Smith
Former England and Warwickshire captain
and ex-England manager

Mike Smith hails the consistency of an umpire who came up through the tough Yorkshire school.

Dickie is a throwback to those days when to play in the Yorkshire Leagues was recognition in the cricket community, a foot on the ladder, the A stream to further honours. That he has become best known for umpiring rather than playing is to miss a point. He has reached the top in the game, and experienced and contributed to it at the highest level.

He couldn't have achieved this without his experience as a player. His background in the game has been a major asset to him. Players have always been aware of the values he attaches to the game of cricket and that, within his capacity, he will see these are maintained and the game is not compromised. All this has helped him to be such a good umpire, which is not all a matter of giving decisions. In addition, players have appreciated his consistency and it always helps to have a bit of 'character' thrown in.

Mike Denness
Former England and Kent captain

———

Now a PR consultant for the Britannic Assurance Championship and National Grid, Mike tells a tale of sixes at Scarborough.

I remember playing for Kent against Yorkshire at Headingley in Dickie's early days as an umpire and Richard Hutton was about to bowl to Stuart Leary, Kent's South African batsman who tragically committed suicide a few years ago by throwing himself off Table Mountain.

Stuart was quite a character and as he waited for Richard to bowl he said to Dickie, 'Just watch out, Dickie, I'm going to hit his first and fifth balls over midwicket for six.'

'I bet you won't,' said Dickie. Richard bowled the first delivery, Stuart swung his bat and the ball sailed out over the leg-side boundary for six. Dickie, all smiles, raised both arms to signal the six.

The next four deliveries were dot balls and as Richard prepared to send down the fifth, Dickie was getting all excited. 'He'll not do it again,' he said. Hutton bowled, Stuart swung ... and over the line it went for another six.

Dickie jumped up and down in excitement. 'Eh, look at that, he's bloody done it,' he said. We couldn't stop laughing. He was like an excited schoolboy. But that was Dickie. He lived every moment out there.

Things always happened when he was out in the middle. There was that occasion when he was appointed the National Grid umpire for the Zimbabwe *v* New Zealand series in 1992 and local officials in Bulawayo were wondering whether the game could go ahead because of a drought. Hose-pipes were banned and the pitch was extremely dry. It hadn't rained properly for five years. It was crisis time.

Enter Dickie. As soon as he got there the heavens opened and a massive storm swept over the ground accompanied by a hurricane. The covers were swept away and the pitch was flooded. 'It could only happen to me,' he said. The farmers were delighted but the cricketers were less pleased.

Graham Gooch
Former captain of England and Essex,
still playing for Essex with a new hairstyle

England's long-serving opener on a painful blow he inflicted on Dickie.

For practically the whole of my career, Dickie has been recognized as one of the best umpires in the world and one who is respected throughout cricket. A real character, he was funny to watch as he jumped around, trying to avoid the ball when it was hit in his direction.

During the 1985 Test series at Old Trafford, England *v* Australia, I hammered a delivery from leg spinner Bob Holland straight back down the track. With no opportunity to get out of the way, Dickie received a fearful crack on the ankle. Down he went, cursing his luck.

'Thanks mate, you saved me four runs there,' said Bob.

After prolonged treatment I ribbed him about robbing me of four runs. He spluttered some unintelligible retort. Cricket will definitely be the loser when he retires from the game.

" *Dickie only wears it when Graham Gooch is batting!* "

Ken Mahood

Keith Fletcher
Former England manager and captain and ex-captain of Essex

'The Gnome', on a day Dickie showed true Yorkshire grit.

Dickie was a very gutsy batsman as he showed when he played against Essex for Leicestershire on a flier of a pitch at Brentwood in 1961. Barry Knight was bowling at the speed of light and made it very uncomfortable for him and his opening partner Maurice Hallam.

Dickie stuck it out despite being hit in the ribs on several occasions. He was very correct and got behind the line; either that or he let it go. Hallam was a different type of player, moving out of the line to pull or cut and though he got more runs, Dickie was the player who impressed us that day. He didn't make many runs, twenty I believe, but he showed true Yorkshire grit. I have to say, though, he was a much better umpire than he was a batter!

Ted Dexter
Former Sussex and England captain and
former chairman of the England Committee

Ted Dexter on the many 'skippers' in Dickie's life.

Dickie always called me 'skipper', even after I had long relin-
quished any captaincy post. I always felt rather flattered. It was
a little while before I realized that Dickie called most cricketers 'skipper'. Collapse of stout party!

Mike Brearley
Former Middlesex and England captain

———

England's most cerebral captain relates a story about how crumbs stopped play in a Test.

At Trent Bridge in 1976, my first Test, the West Indies batted for almost two days with Viv Richards scoring 232. After tea on the second day we did, I am afraid, take things a little slowly. I remember Tony Greig fielding at very deep mid-off at each end. Dickie was at the Pavilion End. He had been driven almost to distraction by the usual delays because of members moving about behind the bowler's arm. As ever, there always seemed to be more when Dickie was at that end.

John Snow added to his problems by filling his pockets with cake crumbs which he quietly scattered at the end of his run. This, of course, attracted the seagulls which swooped noisily and very visibly, holding up play. I think John did this more to tease Dickie than to waste time. Dickie's distress and frantic anxiety was a mixture of real vulnerability and pure theatre. The players – and audiences – have loved him for both.

Dickie is a nervous, amusing and delightful man. I not only respect his umpiring, I also enjoy his company. Umpires are supposed to be calming influences on the players from time to time. I sometimes took that role with him: 'Come on Dickie, relax, it's only a game.'

My only complaint with him was that he required a degree of certainty that is almost neurotic, like that of a man who has to keep going back to the front door to make certain he has locked it. One evening I said to him, half jokingly, 'Dickie, there is no such thing as absolute certainty, only the certainty that befits the subject. What is certain or accurate for a carpenter is not certain or accurate for a geometer.' I did not spell out in too much detail the relevance of Aristotle's point to lbw decisions. I was batting the next day, and I did not want him suddenly to adopt less exacting standards of certainty.

Ken Mahood

Ian Botham
Former England captain and Somerset, Worcestershire
and Durham all-rounder

Dickie and the firecrackers!

I have always reacted badly when umpires have been more concerned about the letter rather than the spirit of the law and that is why my favourite umpire is and always will be Dickie Bird.

Dickie is a complete nutcase of course but a hugely lovable one for the simple reason that you can always have a laugh and a joke with him, as he has proved by his reaction to the catalogue of classic practical jokes to which he has been subjected over the years. My great mate Allan Lamb was quite expert at winding him up. I'll never forget the time we placed firecrackers on Bob Willis's run up during a Test match. When Bob's lumbering strides set them off one by one, Dickie almost had a heart attack because he was convinced he was under attack from crazed gunmen.

Certainly Greg Ritchie and the other Aussies were beside themselves over all the fuss.

Reproduced with permission from Botham, My Autobiography *(Collins Willow 1994).*

Mike Gatting
Former England captain, captain of Middlesex

———

Gatt delivers the verdict from the Pavilion End at Lord's

Very much respected by the touring teams, very animated and colourful, whether moving sightscreens or calling 'Over', or even using a light meter ... that's Dickie. One of the game's characters.

3

THE BATSMEN ...
WHO LIKE HIS STYLE OF UMPIRING!

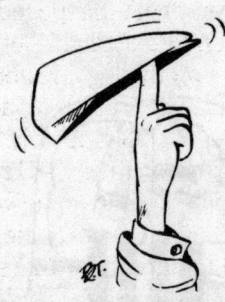

Dickie is universally popular with batsmen. They know if he gives them out then there are no doubts about it. He always gives them the benefit of the doubt.

Raman Subba Row
Former England, Surrey and Northamptonshire batsman
and now ICC Referee

The former TCCB chairman recounts some of Dickie's more hazardous experiences abroad.

I seem to have been the ICC Referee at most of Dickie's matches abroad as a National Grid international umpire. At Hobart in the Australia *v* Pakistan Test he gave David Boon run out in a close decision and, realizing the TV evidence was available, called for it and when it backed his judgement, he said, 'There you are, I knew he was out!'

Dickie's version is slightly different. He claims the equipment wasn't working at the time! He had just arrived in Hobart after a long flight and when the incident happened he called for the third umpire to act, only to be told that the camera had malfunctioned.

'What do I do?' he asked. 'It's your decision,' said the third umpire. So Dickie gave him out. Like all the best cricketing stories, there are a number of versions!

But there was no doubting what happened in the Third Test between the West Indies and Pakistan in Antigua in 1993 when the ball was played square on the legside and Dickie took up a great position level with the crease to adjudicate on any possible run out appeal. Unfortunately for him, Keith Arthurton's throw, a very powerful one as I remember, hit him right at the base of the spine and down he went.

Everyone laughed because it was Dickie, but it was really very painful. He struggled on for a few more minutes until tea and when he stripped off there was an awful-looking bruise on his lower back. 'You can't go back out there like that,' I said. 'You need to put some ice on it and rest up a while.' After a lot of muttering, Dickie agreed and a local umpire, Clancy Mack, was deputed to take over. Mack turned down an lbw appeal by Waqar Younis against Desmond Haynes only to give Brian Lara and Keith Arthurton out lbw on the same score. Richie Richardson was another lbw victim.

There was a local band playing throughout the day's play and they promptly struck up a refrain of 'Bring back, bring back my Dickie to me'. Dickie was not able to oblige that evening and the next day's play was washed out. He was grateful for the rest.

John Edrich
Former Surrey and England batsman and
England batting coach

___

How Dickie gave Dennis Lillee some sound advice ... and made life difficult for 'Edie' and the other England batsmen.

My favourite Dickie story concerns the First Test between England and Australia at Edgbaston in 1975, the infamous occasion when Mike Denness won the toss and put the Aussies in on a dullish morning. The decision backfired as so often happens in Test cricket and the Aussies scored 359.

No sooner had Dennis Amiss and I opened the England innings when a thunderstorm erupted over the ground and we were off the field for nearly two hours. The extra hour had just been added on and it meant we faced almost three hours play in dicey conditions. Dennis Lillee in particular moved the ball all over the place and so did Max Walker. It was a light relief for us when Jeff Thomson came on and sprayed it about.

Lillee struck Dennis Amiss on the elbow and Dennis was feeling sick. Dickie was there to offer sympathy as he always is on these occasions.

That was the Test where Graham Gooch made a pair in his début for England.

I managed to score 34 in England's 101, one of my best innings of its type. One of the first to congratulate me was Dickie, who was standing in the match with Arthur Fagg. 'Great knock lad,' he said. 'But Dennis Lillee wouldn't have got those wickets if I hadn't told him how to bowl in the conditions. He were bowling too short. I told him, you've got to pitch it up more, lad.'

'Thanks very much,' I said. Lillee's figures were 15–8–15–5 and I was left to wonder how different the outcome would have been had he carried on bowling too short! In the second innings it was Thomson, with five wickets, who hastened us to an innings defeat.

Bob Taylor
Former England and Derbyshire wicket-keeper/batsman

———

Bob played against Dickie for many years and his side Derbyshire always seemed to come up with the best practical jokes.

Geoff Miller, my ex-Derbyshire team-mate, was a great practical joker and whenever we played in Scarborough he used to go round to a shop which sold toys and joke items to see what they had with a view to playing a jape.

He was rummaging around one day when he came on a new addition to the stock, capsules which when trodden on made a loud noise. Dickie, who was umpiring the match, was an obvious target.

Geoff spread a few at Dickie's end. When Dickie trod on them there was a loud bang and he jumped up in the air and said, 'What's happening? What's going on?' Everyone roared with laughter and at first Dickie didn't join in. But when it happened an over or two later, he was laughing like the rest of us.

Micky Stewart
Former England manager and Surrey and England batsman

Now the Director of Coaching at the NCA, Micky has seen Dickie in a few embarrassing incidents over the years.

My wife, Sheila, first met Dickie early in his career when Surrey were playing in a game at Yorkshire. Dickie told her he was sailing to Cape Town at the end of the season to take up a coaching post in Johannesburg and was dreading the prospect.

'I hate being in boats,' he said. 'I'm always seasick.' We were there a number of days and a few days later we heard his hilarious account of how he had tried to prepare for the voyage by taking a rowing-boat out on a boating lake near the hotel.

He hired the boat and had a young lad with him to help with the rowing. Unfortunately the wind got up and what was at first a good idea turned out to be a very bad one. Dickie started to panic, complained of feeling ill and told the boy that he was going to jump overboard and make for the shore! And that apparently is what he did. He got out of the boat and waded across the lake to the nearside haven. Luckily for him it wasn't too deep but it left him soaking and sniffling!

Another uproarious Dickie misadventure was in the 1987 World Cup in India when Dickie and David Shepherd were England's umpires. The England squad were staying in the same hotel as the umpires and were readying themselves for the opening banquet.

I saw Shep coming along on his own and asked where Dickie was hiding. 'He's in bed,' he said. 'He's got the runs and won't be able to make it.' Everyone, or nearly everyone, has stomach trouble when they first get to India and Dickie was no exception. Except that he was the first to go down with it.

When I told some of the players they agreed they would have to help the old boy out. We had brought a consignment of food with us, chocolate biscuits, Mars bars and other items, and we took some to his room. 'Get some of this down you, it'll make you feel better,' one of the players told him.

'Aye, but I don't feel like taking anything,' said Dickie. 'It's my stomach. It's terrible.' The sight of the Mars bars cheered him up and he said: 'I might just try one of those.'

As he reached out to pick one up he suffered a convulsion. 'Christ, it's come on again,' he said as he sprinted for the loo. He never did have that Mars bar but, typically of him, he didn't miss the opening ceremony.

In the summer of 1995 I met up with him again when he was umpiring an Under-19 international against South Africa. The boys thought it was marvellous that an umpire of his standing should be officiating in one of their matches. They stood enraptured as he related stories about his experiences with the world's top players.

One of the South African batsmen was on 46 when Dickie suddenly grasped his calf and shouted, 'Hold on, I've pulled a muscle.' There was a slight delay while he rubbed the back of his calf. Next ball the batsman glanced the ball for a boundary to put up what he thought was his fifty.

But to his amazement, Dickie signalled a leg-bye. The batsman must have muttered something about the ball coming off the middle of the bat because Dickie turned to the scorers and shouted, 'Cancel that. Hey, cancel that signal. It were a four off the bat. I was rubbing my bad leg at the time.'

Dennis Amiss

Former England and Warwickshire opening batsman,
now chief executive of Warwickshire

Dickie was standing at the other end when Dennis made some of his biggest scores for England.

Dickie was always happy to break any tension in a game with a little comment or quip. Yet he did not try to impose himself too much on a game. He was always there to talk to but at the same time he did not try to take over. His mannerisms, the way he talked and thought about situations were always quite funny. I am sure he realized this and played on it.

He will always be identified with the bomb scare at Lord's in 1980. I can remember him with his arms on his knees being prepared to go up with the bomb if one went off. All for the sake of a Test wicket at headquarters.

He was always prepared to give you an encouraging word of advice and sometimes he would tell a batsman he was playing really well and was sure to get runs. That was always a big help when you were batting. He was known as a 'not out' umpire which I suppose came from his batting background. You would have to be absolutely plumb on the back foot before he made a decision. That was a little frustrating for a bowler who would be pounding away all day only to find any little doubt going the way of the batsman.

Dickie was very respected and you always knew he was in control of a game. Whatever decision he gave, he knew the laws and you recognized he was in control and there would be no nonsense. He is a lovely man and will be sadly missed when he retires. He will always be welcome at Edgbaston. We have great memories of this tremendous umpire and great character.

Harold Bird walks out with Vic Wilson to open the innings for Yorkshire against the MCC, Scarborough, 1959.

Dickie hits out at The Oval, Leicestershire *v* Surrey, 23 May 1964. The bowler was Ron Tindall.

Dickie shares a joke with Richard Hadlee, England *v* New Zealand, Trent Bridge, June 1990.

Dickie with another great bowler, Bishan Bedi, Brylcreem double wicket international, Wembley 1978.

Dickie in action *(anti-clockwise from top left)*: giving out Clive Lloyd in the World Cup Final, 1975; signalling a wide; giving Carl Hooper run out, England *v* West Indies, Texaco one-day international, Lord's, 1988; another wicket for Imran Khan, Pakistan *v* Australia, Prudential World Cup, Trent Bridge, 1979.

Dickie in trouble *(from top down)*: arguing with a spectator, England *v* New Zealand, The Oval, 1986; Dickie guards the square during a bomb scare at Lord's, England *v* West Indies, 1973; inspecting the covers with Umpire Barry Meyer, England *v* Pakistan, 1987, Old Trafford.

Dickie in a hurry: *(top)* leaving the field during the fifth Test, England *v* West Indies, The Oval, August 1976; *(below)* yet another break for rain during the fourth Test at Old Trafford, England *v* Australia, 1988.

Graham Clinton

Former Kent and Surrey batsman and ex-Surrey first-team coach

_____

Graham relives the time the crowd nearly stopped play.

Players are always teasing Dickie and he nearly always goes along with it. The chat he has with players can brighten a dull day. The story I like most about him concerns Jimmy Adams, the West Indies left-handed batsman from Jamaica.

Jimmy was fielding at square leg close to Dickie in a one-day Texaco Trophy game at the Oval and he kept on at Dickie about the difficult background he faced from the crowd. 'If the ball comes this way I won't see it,' he said. 'All those people with different coloured clothing on! Can't you do something about it?'

Every alternate over Jimmy brought up the subject and Dickie became more and more animated. 'Can't you make them all wear white?' asked Jimmy. Finally Dickie made his mind up and started striding off. Jimmy realized the joke had gone too far. He called out to Dickie. 'Hey, it's only a joke, Dickie!'

Normal relations were immediately restored and everyone had a good laugh.

Alan Oakman
Former England, Sussex and Warwickshire all-rounder

_____

Alan tells the inside story of how Arthur Fagg walked out of a Test match because of sledging.

On the morning of the Second Test between England and the West Indies at Edgbaston in 1973 I was summoned to see Leslie Deakins, the club secretary, and told there was a problem in the umpires' room and I had been asked to attend.

Esmond Kentish, the West Indies manager, Alec Bedser, chairman of the England selectors and Cyril Goodway, chairman of Warwickshire, were in deep conversation when I arrived with Arthur Fagg and Dickie Bird, the two umpires. The problem was that, the night before, Arthur Fagg was upset at the reaction of West Indies skipper Rohan Kanhai when he rejected an appeal for a catch behind the wicket off Geoff Boycott. Arthur was saying he would not continue in the match.

That morning the *Daily Mail* and *Sun* carried bold headlines stating that Arthur was resigning and walking out of the match. While the discussions were going on Dickie was sitting in his vest and pants twiddling with his forelock and earnestly trying to convince Arthur that he had to continue. 'Tha' can't let the spectators down, tha' can't do it, Arthur,' he said. He started cavorting around the room, slightly stooping, elbows outwards, like he has done in Test matches.

By now time was running out and the start of play at eleven-thirty was not far away. I could see Dickie was getting more and more agitated. Arthur was adamant that he wouldn't go out for the start as he felt the players' attitude towards umpires over the previous few years had deteriorated and a stand had to be made. Following further discussions, it was agreed that he would not stand for the first over and the public would be made aware of that and I would stand for the first over at square leg.

I looked across at Dickie and he had a look of relief on his face. The five-minute bell went and we got ready to go out. As we walked out onto the pitch I realized I had forgotten the bails. As a joke, I said to Dickie, 'I've had second thoughts about this. I don't see why I should come out for one over and I'm going off.'

The look on Dickie's face will live with me for the rest of my life. He turned towards me, shoulders stooped more than ever, hands on hips, elbows pointing backwards and said, 'Oakie, tha' can't, tha' can't, what am I going to do?' I said, 'I couldn't care less,' and turned towards the dressing room. He started walking after me and I placated him by saying, 'Don't worry Dickie, I'm just going to get the bails. I forgot them.'

If ever a man was relieved! 'Hurry up Oakie,' he said. 'It hasn't been a very good day for me so far.' By now the West Indians were coming out and Rohan said, 'Where are you going?' I said the same to him and he looked in utter disbelief. I turned to Lance Gibbs and said, 'I've forgotten the bails.' Lance saw the funny side of it.

Every year since, when Dickie has come to Edgbaston he has mentioned this affair and I can still picture him sitting in the dressing room in his underclothes, twiddling his forelock and jumping up and down. He always likes coming to Edgbaston because he likes going to Sir Harry's fish and chip shop nearby. 'Best in country,' he always says, 'outside Yorkshire.'

Why he has never gone completely grey I shall never know!

Phil Sharpe
Ex-Yorkshire and England

One of Dickie's former playing colleagues on a double run-out.

Dickie is indeed in love with cricket which is why he never married but I can reveal he came close to it in South Africa. The girl's name was Beverley and he was extremely keen on her at the time. I can vouch for that!

One of the funnier moments was at the Oval when I was playing for Yorkshire and he was umpiring and I played the ball straight past the bowler and called for a single. It was one of those when there was some hesitation over taking a second. Finally we did and the fielder who had retrieved the ball shied at the bowler's end, hitting and taking the bails off and the ball ran on down the pitch to hit the stumps at the end I was running towards.

There was an appeal and Dickie was instantly in one of his 'rather concerned' states. The players thought it was very funny because Dickie hadn't expected to be involved. It should have been the other umpire. But he made the right decision; I was given out and it all ended happily.

Nasser Hussain
Essex and England batsman

The England A team captain on how he was 'stone dead' out at Old Trafford.

We were playing against Lancashire at Old Trafford and Paul Prichard had this theory about Wasim Akram's outswinger. He said you could tell when he was going to bowl it by the way his arm came over.

Dickie was at Wasim's end and I'd made about ten when I shouldered arms for what I thought was the outswinger only to discover it was the one that went the other way. I was plumb in front and Dickie raised the finger.

'Sorry, old lad,' he said, 'but you were stone dead.' I didn't say anything and I must have looked a bit miserable because Dickie made a point of coming up to me in the showers to talk about it. 'Sorry, old mate,' he said. 'It were stone dead. Stone dead.'

I wasn't complaining. 'Don't worry,' I said. 'Would have hit middle. Never any doubt.'

'Aye,' said Dickie. 'That's all right then. But it were stone dead, y'know!'

Alec Stewart
Surrey and England

Alec shares with Dickie a love of football.

I will miss the chats I always have with Dickie when he is at square leg and I am fielding on that side of the wicket. They are always about football. He knows I am a Chelsea fan and he talks about Barnsley, his local club, and Sheffield Wednesday.

He is a rotten forecaster. Most years he will say to me, 'With the team you've got here, you'll win something.' He hasn't been right yet!

I can't remember an occasion when he has given me out and I have been unhappy about it. As a batsman, you are always glad to see he is umpiring. As a person, he's tremendous. I have always enjoyed playing when he has been officiating.

Surrey were playing Somerset at Weston-super-Mare a few years back and it was Red Nose Day. David Ward, our short-leg fielder, was wearing a red nose under his helmet. Dickie took a little time to notice it but when he did, he burst out laughing. 'What's going on here then?' he said. After a short while he told David to take it off. 'Can't have that, lad,' he said.

Dickie always seems to be in bother about bad light but he is right to be on the cautious side. You never know when some-one is going to hit the ball back at you and you can't see it in time. He's had a few near misses and it happened to me once when Monte Lynch drove one back and it hit me on the foot. The umpires are in the front line.

Bill Tidy

John Steele
Former Leicestershire batsman

Dickie's parking problems at Grace Road.

Whenever Dickie umpired at Grace Road, Leicester, he would ask me if he could park his car in my driveway. I lived at Park Hill Avenue, a short walk from the ground.

He had a sponsored car in those days, with his name 'Dickie Bird – Test Match Umpire' emblazoned on the door. 'They keep writing things on it,' he complained. 'They take the mick all the time. Can't leave it anywhere.'

David Steele
Former Northants, Derby and England batsman

'The straightest bat in England' on how Dickie saved him from being timed out at Lord's.

I shall always be grateful to Dickie because he saved my bacon on my Test début at Lord's in 1975. I was next to go in but got lost in the pavilion. Instead of turning into the Long Room and going out through the centre door, I carried on down the stairs and found myself in the basement toilets.

Out in the middle the Australians were going frantic. Ian Chappell, the skipper, was getting on at Dickie. 'Where is he?' he said. 'You'll have to time him out, Dickie.'

But to his credit Dickie held firm and it must have been at least four minutes before I was able to take guard. The law only allows two of course. I managed to go on and make fifty so I had a lot to thank Dickie for. Dickie wouldn't give you out on the front foot, particularly if the ball was moving about, so he was ideal for me.

Max Walker got very upset because whenever he hit me on the front pad and went up Dickie would shake his head and say, 'Not out!' After several of these unsuccessful appeals, Max said to him, 'Bloody hell, Dickie. What's going on?' 'You're bowling from too wide, man,' said Dickie.

Later on Max found the pad again with a big in ducker, appealed and Dickie said, 'Not out.' Max started muttering and Dickie walked to the side of the crease and scuffed his foot. 'You're bowling from out here and that's too wide,' he said.

Dickie was a grand lad, a very honest person and he set the scene for umpires in recent years. He is a character but was good enough at his job to come into prominence and show everyone he's a character. If you're like that in the second team you'll never get heard of.

We always had a lot of fun with him. In one game at Northants Peter Lee was bowling and 'Leapy' used to spend a lot of time picking the seam. He bowled, the batsman got a nick and I cut my finger catching the ball at second slip ... because the seam was so high. Bill Alley was standing with Dickie and said, 'Let's have a look at that ball.'

Someone threw it to him and he called Dickie over. Bill was a bowler who used to work the seam himself when he was a player and he held the ball up admiringly and said to Leapy, 'If you don't get 7–29 with that I'll report you!' I came on to bowl and thought I'd continue the good work but Dickie spotted me. 'What are you up to?' he asked. 'I'm just cleaning the seam,' I replied. Dickie looked reprovingly and said, 'Well make sure you do it behind my back so I can't see you!'

Another story I remember about Dickie happened in a Sunday League game when I was playing for Derbyshire. I was having trouble with no-balls and someone suggested I borrow Colin Tunnicliffe's size fourteens which would help me to get part of my boot on the line. The boots were such a bad fit that I couldn't move around too well in them and the other players had to carry me down the steps of the pavilion.

As I prepared to bowl, Dickie said, 'What are those?' 'They're my anti-no-ball boots,' I said. Dickie called his fellow umpire Arthur Jepson over. 'What do you think of this?' he said. 'Is it all right?' I didn't bowl too many no-balls after that and everyone had a good laugh. I never took those Sunday League matches too seriously. They're not proper cricket.

David Lloyd
Former Lancashire and England batsman, now
Lancashire head coach and England coach

———

*How Dickie thought he was about to be bitten by a snake at the
luncheon table.*

Dickie was always a prime candidate for a jape and starred in
one of the best ones we've ever had at Old Trafford. It
happened in the early Eighties when Mick Malone, an
Australian who was a great practical joker, turned up with a
very lifelike rubber snake.

He primed a waitress in the players' dining room to serve
Dickie a special lunch on one of those plates with a silver
dome cover. She went to Dickie's table and told him that the
chef had something special for his lunch.

'Ee, thanks very much, luv,' said Dickie as he picked up his
knife and fork. 'I were feeling a bit peckish.'

The dome came off and the snake unravelled on the plate.
Dickie shrieked, and literally flew out of the dining room,
down the pavilion steps and across the outfield to the middle
of the square where he sat down and flatly refused to set foot
in the pavilion again. We could hear him from the players'
balcony. 'There's a snake in theer, running loose, running
loose it is, aye, in that dining room, don't go in!'

Phil Neale
Former Worcestershire batsman and
current Warwickshire manager

Phil on the day Dickie forgot to call 'No-ball'.

They used to love him when I played at Worcester. He had a great rapport with the players and they were always ribbing him and having a bit of fun. Not that too many of the bowlers wanted to bowl at his end! In those days he had a reputation for never giving anyone out lbw.

In one match John Inchmore, the medium-fast bowler, was bowling and Dickie was fussing about him running down the pitch. Dickie would make a point of walking down the pitch and pointing. 'You can't do that, lad,' he kept saying.

John was getting a bit uppity about it and next ball he suddenly changed sides and bowled round the wicket instead of over. Dickie was almost apoplectic. 'What are you doing, man?' he said. 'You can't do that. It's not allowed. What do you think you're up to?'

John laughed and we all joined in. Technically speaking Dickie should have called, 'No-ball', but in the excitement he forgot. He kept on talking about it for the rest of the session.

Andy Moles
Warwickshire batsman

Dickie's awkward moment with Norman Gifford.

There are loads of stories about Dickie but the one I like best is the time he was standing in a game and Norman Gifford, then with Worcestershire, was bowling. I can't remember who the batsman was but he wasn't ready and as Giff ran in Dickie held his arm out to stop him bowling.

Giff didn't take any notice. He kept coming and ducked under Dickie's arm and bowled. The batsman was a bit surprised and missed it. He wasn't out but Dickie was upset.

"Ere Giff,' he said. 'What do you think you're up to? You can't do that. You'll have to bowl that one again.'

Giff put on a bit of an act. 'I'm paid to bowl six balls an over and that was one of them,' he said. 'You'll not get me to bowl another one.'

'That's not right,' said Dickie. 'Start again.' But Giff wouldn't give way. 'That's my delivery and I'm sticking by it,' he said. I think Dickie had to accept it eventually.

Then there was another famous occasion when Dickie was taken short out in the middle. I don't know whether he'd had a curry the night before or what. But he suddenly doubled up and said, 'Skipper, I've got to go off for a moment or two.'

We were in stitches. Off he went and someone else had to come on for ten minutes or so and stand at square leg.

4

THE BOWLERS ...
WHO ARE MORE COMPLAINING

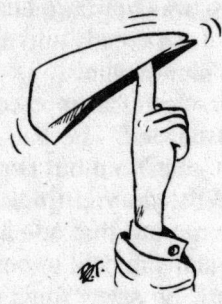

Bowlers have their reservations about Dickie's umpiring because they believe he never gives them an inch. Any deviation, any margin at the line, he calls it in the batsman's favour.

Chris Old
Former Yorkshire and England bowler

Now coaching in Cornwall, Chris explains how a tower block stopped play at the Oval and threw Dickie into a tizz!

One of the big dramas of Dickie's career was the occasion when the sun's reflection caused the abandonment of play in the England *v* Pakistan Test at the Oval in 1974. Sarfraz was bowling and I was the batsman. It was six-fifteen in the evening on a brilliantly sunny day and I was being blinded by a reflection off the Shell Building about a mile away. It may seem unbelievable but it was true.

'What do I do?' asked Dickie. 'I can't ask them to close the window, can I?' Intikhab, the Pakistan captain, stood on the batting crease and looked towards the Vauxhall End and had to admit I was right. Like me, he was being blinded by the reflected light. After a short delay, we all trooped off to the pavilion. The spectators were totally bewildered.

Dickie always had to be sure when he gave a batsman out lbw. I remember in a Test against the West Indies at Edgbaston I was bowling to Clive Lloyd and the ball hit him on the pad, right in front. I appealed but as I looked round at Dickie he didn't appear to be about to give Lloyd out. I sank slowly to my knees with an imploring expression on my face. I could see he was unsure.

After what seemed an eternity he raised his arm and said, 'That's out.' Later that night I saw him again and he said: 'Did you see the replay? It were out, weren't it? Did you see it?' I reassured him that it did indeed look out and, as usual, he had made the right decision. He wanted perfection and often I reckon he achieved it. Half the time I couldn't understand what he was saying. He kept jabbering away and fidgeting about.

I was the bowler when Dickie made what he often says was his best decision. It happened in the Old Trafford Test against India in 1974 when Viswanath had just passed fifty in the final twenty overs and the Indians appeared to be on their way to victory. I bowled on the line of leg stump and it went down the legside for Alan Knott to take and make a loud appeal. I didn't appeal myself because I didn't think it had touched the bat. Vishy, who always walked, stood his ground and looked appealingly at Dickie, who proceeded to raise the finger. Vishy looked very unhappy and the Indians went on to lose five wickets for 43 and with them, the match. Dickie saw Vishy afterwards and asked him what he thought about his decision. 'Sorry Mr Dickie,' said Vishy. 'It just flicked my glove and you were right but I had to stand there because I was fighting to save my country.'

"If you won't wear a hat I'll have to take the players off!"

Ken Mahood

Dickie was officiating when I scored a hundred in thirty-seven minutes against Warwickshire at Edgbaston in 1987 and came within two minutes of equalling Percy Fender's record for the fastest first-class hundred. As most of the bowling was delivered by non-bowlers who were intent on improving Warwickshire's over rate it wouldn't have counted anyway but Dickie kept encouraging me. 'You'll do it,' he said. 'You don't have to take risks.'

He was one of the first umpires to make a stand about bowlers running down the wicket. He would walk down the pitch and shift his feet about, looking intently at the ground. Sometimes he never said a word but you got the message. Well, he probably did say a few words but I couldn't understand him!

Another time I was involved in an incident with Dickie was in 1981 at Derby the first year the regulation was introduced about having four fielders within the circle in Benson and Hedges games. Derbyshire's Barry Wood was bowling and I noticed there were only three men inside the circle. I took a swing and was bowled and the Derbyshire players were rather surprised I made no effort to leave the pitch. 'I can't be out, they didn't have four men in the ring,' I said. Geoff Boycott, batting at the other end, agreed with me and the umpires, Dickie and Arthur Jepson, conferred.

'Let's keep calm, gentlemen,' said Dickie, who was not the calmest man around himself. After a short debate, the umpires decided the only solution was to ring Lord's and get a ruling. Whoever they spoke to said I could carry on batting providing another delivery hadn't been bowled. It didn't make much difference. I was out almost immediately afterwards.

David Graveney
Former Gloucestershire and Durham spin bowler

_____

The chief executive of the Professional Cricketers' Association reveals his side of a more unusual story about Dickie.

I must be one of the few cricketers who have clashed with Dickie. It happened in a zonal match of the Benson and Hedges Cup at Chesterfield in 1985. I was captain of Gloucestershire and when Derby batted it was a bright, sunny day at first and they scored 202–7 in their 55 overs. It clouded over when we batted and it became pretty obvious that the game wouldn't end. It was going to be difficult to get in the 20 overs that needed to be bowled if the match was shortened and the side with the faster run rate was going to go through.

We needed just one point to qualify for the first time for ages and I was getting a bit upset that Dickie and his fellow umpire John Jameson kept the game going when the light was getting too bad. Dickie insisted that we had to stay out there until 20 overs had been bowled and I disagreed. Derbyshire did bowl 20.2 overs before it was decided to come off and as they had the faster rate over the first 20 overs, they went through.

We took it up at Lord's and as a result, the rules were rewritten and umpires were instructed that if a result wasn't possible on the first day it should be treated like a two-day match. It rained on the second day at Chesterfield and play was washed out. Dickie is always a stickler about going off for light – he used to get himself in a right flap about it – but on that occasion he was the opposite!

We were still good friends afterwards. We didn't let it worry us. I have a lot of respect for him. He was always encouraging me. He would say, 'You're bowling beautifully. You're the best left-arm spinner in the country.' It gave you an injection of confidence just when you needed it.

He was saying the same sort of thing to the other players. He wasn't biased. No, he's a lovely bloke and though I did have that difference of opinion with him our relationship was never affected.

I have to say this about Dickie: he enforced Law 42, section 8, better than any other umpire in my experience. That is the law regarding intimidatory bowling. He never shirked from the battle which was remarkable for someone who was shy by nature. Courtney Walsh rates him the best and he is not the only one.

Jack Simmons
Former Lancashire and Tasmanian all-rounder

How Dickie coached one of English cricket's most accurate bowlers and enabled him to get the odd lbw decision.

I got to know Dickie very well on a coaching trip to South Africa in 1971 and we became firm friends. We still are despite the fact he never responded to my lbw appeals! We coached at schools and during term time Dickie would have his lunch at the school. But during the holidays he would come to my house and my wife Jacqueline would give him his lunch. Some of the other coaches used to rib him. 'You sure you've paid for that?' they'd say.

He had just started his umpiring career the year before when I played in a match for Lancashire where he was standing. He turned down a few appeals for lbw saying I was bowling too wide of the crease. That winter he coached me in the nets to solve the problem and I was very grateful to him.

The following season Lancashire were playing Middlesex and I remembered what he had said about my line. 'Pitch it on off and don't turn it, and if you don't turn it, you've got a chance,' he said. Mike Brearley was the batsman and I pitched straight, the ball hit him on the back foot and in my view would have hit all three. But to my amazement Dickie gave him not out. I asked him why and he said, 'You've done everything right except for one thing. You've stood right in front of me and I can't see the batsman!'

I think he was probably right because other umpires around that time told me I was obscuring their view and it was something I had to work on to correct. Later on, when he became established, I told him our house was always available for him to stay at when he was officiating at Old Trafford and he readily accepted the offer. 'That's very good of you,' he said. After the first time he stayed, he said, 'How much do I owe you?' I said, 'Don't be silly Dickie, you're a guest, a friend of the family.'

'What about the wife?' he said. 'Would she like a bunch of flowers?' I said that would be a good idea. But I think he must have forgotten because they failed to arrive!

He used to drive a sponsored car, not a very prestigious vehicle, and one day I said to him, 'Someone like you, the best umpire in the world, ought to be driving a top of the range Jag or Merc. You shouldn't be riding around in that.'

The next time I saw him he said, 'I've taken your advice. It's not a Jag, but it's a Rover, a big 'un. I've got to have a bit of comfort at my age.' I saw him again later that season and he was complaining about his new car. 'Broke down on the M1,' he said. 'Caused me all kinds of problems. It's all your fault. Once you get talked into doing things you know aren't right you get problems!' I understand he now drives a medium-size car.

Min Patel
Kent and England A spin bowler

———

*How Dickie helped one of our more promising young bowlers ...
and then 'fingered' him.*

I was playing for Kent Seconds in a game at Canterbury.
Dickie was standing in it. It's not uncommon for Test umpires
to do the occasional second team match. I was just starting my
career and I felt it was an honour just being on the same pitch
as Dickie.

He never stopped talking when he was at square leg and I
was fielding on that side. He was full of stories about things
that had happened to him. And he spent quite a lot of time
giving me encouragement.

'There's not a lot wrong with your action,' he said. 'Just keep
working at it and you'll get somewhere in this game.' I thought
it was fantastic that someone of his standing should want to be
so friendly to a young newcomer.

A few years later I was playing against the South Africans at
Canterbury and Hansie Cronje was bowling. I missed his first
delivery, the first ball I faced, and Hansie appealed for lbw.
'That's out,' said Dickie as he raised the finger. About that time
he was giving them! I knew I was out. If he gave me out, I was
out.

Geoff Arnold
Former Surrey and England bowler and England coach

———————

The occasion when Dickie failed to take action against intimidatory bowling.

Dickie has always been ready to step in and warn a bowler for using intimidatory tactics and a number of the world's leading bowlers, including Malcolm Marshall, Dennis Lillee and Courtney Walsh, have been told to 'space 'em out' when bowling short-pitched deliveries.

But there was an occasion at the Oval in June, 1977, when I was pleased Dickie didn't intervene. David Brown, the Warwickshire captain, set Surrey a target of 235 in about 150 minutes on a typically flat Oval pitch and our skipper John Edrich decided to go for it. He promoted me to six in the order and I began middling the ball from the start. Brownie brought back Bob Willis and the shorter Bob bowled, the harder I hit him out of the ground. I remember driving him over extra cover for six in one over and when he dropped one short I pulled it out into the road in the direction of Archbishop Tenison's School.

Bob was livid and kept bowling halfway down the pitch. As the hook shot was one of my specialities I didn't mind a bit. But I could see Dickie was becoming agitated.

I thought I would rib him. 'What about these short-pitched deliveries?' I shouted down the pitch. 'The way you're hitting them out of the ground I'd say you're not too bothered, are you?' he said. At the end of the over I was at his end and I told him, 'I'm glad you haven't done anything about it. It's my finest shot.' I scored 56 in 32 balls and poor Bob had figures of 0–44 in seven overs. We won with seven balls to spare. Things might have been different though had Dickie been officious.

In my experience, he never was. He sensed what was happening in games and used his common sense.

Fred Titmus
Former Middlesex and England off-spin bowler and
current Test selector

H. D. Bird, student of the game.

Dickie was just starting his umpiring career when I was playing and he was a pleasure to play with and you could see he
was on his way to the top. It was different in those days. The
pressure wasn't so great and players could chat to the umpires
more informally. It wasn't such a volatile game, although there
were a few exceptions.

Every umpire makes mistakes but Dickie made fewer than
most. He had a sound Yorkshire upbringing. He studied
bowlers and their actions and he also studied batsmen. He
knew the game.

He was probably more dedicated to his job than his rivals.
He wasn't so eccentric in those days!

Jonathan Agnew
Former Leicestershire and England bowler

The BBC's cricket correspondent on the day nuclear fallout hit Grace Road.

The match was Leicestershire *v* Kent at Grace Road in April 1986, our opening game of the season, and Dickie was officiating along with fellow Yorkshireman Barrie Leadbeater. It was a typically cold and miserable start to the season.

A few days before, the nuclear disaster had occurred at Chernobyl in Russia and everyone was talking about what effect it would have on European countries. No-one was taking it too seriously except Dickie.

Flat cap pulled down over his eyes, he gazed up to the leaden skies and said, 'Nuclear fallout, lad. It's coming. It's on its way.'

Fortunately it never came. I remember what happened in the match – I took 5–27 as we bowled Kent out for 85. But the weather shortened the game and it ended in a draw. Dickie was still going on about nuclear fallout when it ended!

Richard Illingworth
Worcestershire and England slow bowler

———

Richard describes how Dickie talked him through his maiden first-class century.

Dickie was standing in the county match when I scored my first championship hundred so I'll never forget him. I'm a Yorkshireman and I think he has a soft spot for his fellow Yorkshiremen.

As I got closer, he kept saying, 'Keep going lad, you'll not have me giving you out! You've got nothing to fear at this end!'

He was joking but there weren't any close calls as I remember. I finished with 120 not out, my career best. The match was against Warwickshire at New Road. Dickie was one of the first to congratulate me.

Dominic Cork
Derbyshire and England all-rounder

England's leading all-rounder on his first wicket for England.

I'll always remember Dickie because he was the umpire who gave me my first wicket in international cricket. It was in a Texaco Trophy one-day international at Old Trafford on 24 August 1992. The batsman was Inzaman-Ul-Haq and he was on 75. I think it had to be out if Dickie gave it! Yes it was, no doubts. Dickie always has to be sure before he gives anyone out.

He is very conscientious and fair and always has been.

Angus Fraser
Middlesex and England

You can always have a frank exchange with Dickie, says one of England's most loyal performers with the ball.

My foremost memory of Dickie was the occasion at Lord's when I was bowling in a championship match and I appealed for lbw and he said, 'Bugger off!' I was a little surprised but he is the kind of umpire you can have that relationship with because he's always talking and giving the impression that he's enjoying it.

I suppose it was a bit of a hopeful appeal! It takes the pressure off when someone like that is out there. You can always have a laugh and a joke with him. You can talk to most of them but he's the most chatty. 'Well bowled,' he will say and it makes you feel a bit better.

The other outstanding memory I have of him is the time I was playing in a Test at Headingley against the West Indies and he accidentally fell over. The link up with the third umpire came out of his chest pocket or wherever he had it wired up and he was in an awful panic. We were all falling about laughing.

Dean Headley
Kent, Middlesex and England A

The time when Dickie saw the error of his ways and changed a decision.

The game was Kent *v* Northants at Canterbury and Curtly Ambrose was bowling to Graham Cowdrey. Curtly bowled a short one, Graham tried to hit it, appeared to miss and the ball went through to the keeper who caught it.

There was a concerted appeal and Dickie signalled out. Graham was livid. He waved his arms about and said the ball came off his shoulder. As he walked away, he carried on waving his bat about and muttering about being given out when he hadn't touched the ball.

Dickie looked very concerned. When Graham was halfway off to the pavilion he suddenly said, 'I'm calling him back, skipper. I think I've made a mistake.'

It was Allan Lamb's turn to be livid. 'You gave him out,' he said. 'Aye,' said Dickie. 'I know. But I think I got it wrong.' Graham got the message and started to return to the crease. What Lambie said was unprintable. But Dickie stuck to his guns. There aren't many top-class umpires big enough to say they've made a mistake but he's one.

Fred Trueman
The Greatest Living Yorkshireman, arguably!

The great England bowler on the time a half-crown held everyone up at Johannesburg airport.

About five years ago I went on a speaking tour of South Africa with my wife, Veronica, Ian Botham and his wife, Kath, and Dickie. We were held up arriving for a flight from Johannesburg to Durban but when we got to the airport we found the plane was still waiting for us. It meant we had to clear formalities quickly and Veronica and I and the Bothams whisked through the security checks.

Not so Dickie. The first time he passed the magic eye the buzzer went and he had to go back. A man frisked him. 'I've got nowt in my pockets,' he said. 'I've got no idea what it can be.'

'Come on, Dickie,' said Both. 'We'll miss the flight.' Dickie tried again. Once more the buzzer went. They checked him over again. Nothing.

'Goodness me, Dickie, get on with it,' said Veronica. Dickie tried a third time. The same result. This time they gave him the extra special frisk ... and discovered an old half-crown hidden away in the lining of his blazer! Incidentally, we managed to catch the plane. He's a super lad.

Jim Cumbes

The former Lancashire, Surrey, Worcestershire and
Warwickshire bowler and ex-Tranmere, WBA and
Aston Villa goalkeeper

Dickie's problems with the nip-backers.

The time was the mid-Seventies and I was playing for
Worcestershire against Surrey at the Oval. I had been bowling
a rather longish spell in the afternoon when suddenly in one
over I had three strong appeals for lbw against Graham Roope.
Naturally, as a bowler, I felt all three were out but certainly
when the last one was turned down I was feeling pretty peeved
at the umpire, who happened to be Dickie.

Dickie and I had always got on pretty well and never had a
cross word despite the fact I always caused him a few
problems with my follow through which was close to running
on the wicket. In fact, on one occasion I received a final public
warning from him!

After the third appeal, from the sixth and last ball of the
over, I wandered back dejectedly towards him to take my
sweater and as I did so, I said to him half jokingly, 'When are
you going to give me an lbw Dickie? I don't think I've had one
off you in the whole of my career!'

His reply was, 'Jimmy, they were all nip-backers lad and tha'
can't get lbws wi' nip-backers! Now if you hold one up [a leg-
cutter for the uninitiated] then you've got a chance!' I had
become totally frustrated and nodded in the direction of the
huge gasometer next to the ground. 'I reckon if he was in front
of that bloody gasometer you wouldn't give him out, Dickie,' I
said.

'Not if it were a nip-backer, Jimmy lad, not if it were a nip-
backer,' he said. Close fielders and the non-striking batter
burst into gales of laughter. And I have to admit, I laughed
myself.

Ray East
Former Essex spin bowler

'I spent most of my career on my knees appealing to Dickie,' says one of the game's leading characters.

I was the only bowler in the country who used to regularly sink to his knees, arms upraised, to appeal to Dickie for an lbw. That was because he would never give me one. 'Left arm over, you've got to straighten it, lad,' he would say. As for anything on the front foot, no chance. They had to be right back on their stumps. If it was me bowling, forget it!

Then one day at Chelmsford, just as I was giving up on him, I hit this batsman on the pad and sank slowly to my knees to appeal, more in hope than in earnest. It looked plumb to me. But so had so many others. This time Dickie raised the finger, almost triumphantly. 'That's out!' he said.

I jumped up to celebrate. 'Aye, that were plumb,' he said. 'It straightened.'

I had a lot of fun with Dickie over the years. He had this peculiar backwards run when he was retreating for a possible run out and I copied it.

In 1983 he was standing quite close at square leg when Dallas Moir of Derbyshire was bowling to Kenny McEwan. Dallas dropped one short and Kenny pulled it like a tracer bullet towards Dickie. Poor Dickie couldn't get out of the way and it caught him on the right shin. 'Feels like my leg is broken,' he said. A big lump appeared and it was obvious he would have to leave the field.

In another game Kenny won a magnum of champagne from a national newspaper and we arranged for twelfth man Keith Pont to bring out a bottle with the appropriate glasses at the next drinks interval. I cracked open the bottle and offered Dickie the first glass.

Bill Tidy

John Lever
The former Essex and England bowler

Dickie was always concerned about how much money players were making from their benefits.

There was always plenty of chit-chat when Dickie umpired our matches. It was part of his charm. He always wanted to know what was happening and never let the tension affect his decisions. He would only get stroppy with things off the field, like spectators moving about behind the arm.

One of the subjects he always talked about was benefits. He never had one himself and nor did his friend Jack van Geloven who stood with him in many matches. 'Did you see what so-and-so got in his benefit?' he would ask. 'Did you see? Good Lord, man, what's it coming to?'

Phil Tufnell
Middlesex and England spin bowler

Tuffers on his favourite umpire.

Dickie is the umpire I get on with best. I shall be sorry when
he goes.

Pat Pocock
Former Surrey and England off-spin bowler

————

On Dickie's oddball behaviour as the plane for Johannesburg took off.

It is an unforgettable experience flying with Dickie. I had the experience some years ago when we were both coaching at the Wanderers in Johannesburg. Dickie has a loud voice and he could be heard at the terminal at Heathrow going on about how he hated flying.

He made sure he had a seat right at the back of the Boeing 707. 'Always do that,' he said. I asked him why, to lead him on. 'You never get a pilot reversing a plane into a mountain, do you?' he replied.

When we boarded, he made a fuss of getting the seat he wanted at the back and the minutes before take-off were like a one-man virtuoso performance. He never stopped talking and as the plane roared down the runway and reached the point where the pilot gives it lift-off he jumped to his feet, arms waving and shouted, 'Take her up there!'

I'm not sure he still does that. He's a one off, is Dickie!

Peter Lever
Former Lancashire and England bowler and
England bowling coach

The 1975 season was one of the hottest on record but it just had to be Dickie who was involved in a snow stops play incident!

I played in that match at Buxton in 1975 when it snowed, one of the first times in the history of cricket snow stopped play. Clive Lloyd was the Lancashire captain and he'd never seen a snowflake before.

On the way to the ground we drove through an unbelievable blizzard which reduced visibility to fifty yards. No-one disagreed with Dickie when he said, 'We'll not be playing here today!' It was three inches deep in some places.

On the first day Lancashire scored 477–5 in 100 overs, up to then the highest score since the 100-overs limitation took effect. Clive scored an unbeaten 167 in the same number of minutes.

After the wash-out on the second day, the game resumed on a flier of a pitch on the last day. Every time the ball landed it ripped out a divot and reared up and this was before they used helmets! The only way you could hit the stumps was to pitch it up in the block hole which explained why only one batsman was bowled as Derbyshire were shot out for 42 and 87.

The Derbyshire number five batsman was Ashley Harvey Walker, a big lad who looked ashen faced when he arrived at the crease. He took a glove off, fumbled around in his mouth and extracted a set of false teeth.

'Here Dickie,' he said. 'Can you look after these, I don't want them damaged.' Dickie was aghast. 'I'm not putting those in my pocket,' he said. 'They don't look clean to me.'

After a bit of discussion, Dickie promised to take the offending teeth providing they were wrapped up. Ashley pulled out a hankie and duly wrapped them up.

David Lloyd was fielding at bat pad and said, 'Hang on a minute, if you're going to look after his, Dickie, you can look after mine!' So he took his false set out and handed them over. 'You've got a full set now, Dickie, lad,' said one of the other players.

The first ball Ashley faced took off and flicked his ear as it went through to the wicket-keeper Faroukh Engineer. The next ball also lifted and was heading straight for his face when he shot up a hand and it bounced into the air. He turned his head away and didn't see what happened to it after that. But Lloydie caught it.

'Have you caught it?' Ashley said to Lloydie. 'Of course I have,' said David. 'Now take your teeth and clear off!'

It was a miracle that no-one was hurt. We played on un-covered pitches in those days and you needed a good tech-nique to survive. I'll be sorry when Dickie eventually goes. He is a natural comedian who has made a great contribution to our cricket. They can now throw away the mould he came from because there will never be any like him again.

Dennis Lillee
Former Australian fast bowler

———

No-one better than Dickie, says his No.1 admirer Down Under.

Harold Dennis Dickie Bird! The name was enough to intrigue me when we first met as umpire and player but it certainly did not indicate the nature of this great official and great man.

Dickie is the ideal umpire, one who played the game at county level and has a genuine understanding of the people he is controlling during each game. He knows when to talk to the players, when to joke with them and when and how to discipline them. But above all, he has the ability to make correct decisions. Then there is the other side of the person and that is the man. His dry humour has always amused me and I will quote an example.

At the Oval during the 1975 Australian tour of England I requested a change of a rather battered ball which was out of shape. Dickie looked at it, handed it back and told me to complete the over. I wasn't happy with this as the ball was definitely not up to the expected standard for a Test. I could not hope to work miracles with it so I threw it across to the captain Ian Chappell. He said, 'I realize it is out of shape but complete the over with it and I will have a chat to Dickie.'

That didn't suit me, either, so I protested by delivering three good length, well flighted offspinners, telling Dickie in no uncertain terms that the ball could be used only by the slower men.

His serious reaction and dead straight face merely masked his thoughts for when Ian came up at the end of the over to bargain for a better ball, Dickie said, 'I wouldn't change either the ball or the bowler. He's the best off-spinner I have seen all season!' Being the fair and reasonable man he is, though, he immediately met our request and another ball was provided.

Dickie recounts the story of how I told him in that match that I was about to bowl an off-cutter which would rap the batsman on the pads. 'I'll be up for an appeal, you watch,' I said.

Well, it was an off-cutter, it did strike the pads and I did launch myself into a loud appeal. But Dickie spoiled it by saying, 'Not out.'

Whenever I had a word or two with batsmen, he would let me know that he did not approve, saying, 'Come on, Dennis, get on with your bowling.'

Dickie was also one of my main supporters, describing me as the best fast bowler he had umpired. In turn, I think he was the best umpire I came across in England.

Reproduced with permission from Not Out *by Dennis Lillee (Arthur Barker, 1985).*

Sir Richard Hadlee

Former New Zealand and Nottinghamshire all-rounder

Dickie acted as my motivator, says New Zealand's finest bowler.

When I think of umpires I have been involved with, England's Dickie Bird is unquestionably the first who comes to mind. He is one of umpiring's great characters, as much a personality as any player. But he is not merely an infectious character, he is undoubtedly the best umpire in the world and enjoys enormous respect from most players. He's nervous and fidgety and is instantly recognizable by the little idiosyncrasies and gestures which are part of his make-up. He is totally aware of these outward signs of nervousness and has said of them, 'I am highly strung. All my mannerisms come out of me when I am on the field, and this helps me to unwind when I am in the middle.'

As an umpire, he is an outstanding operator. To me, he is someone special, one of those umpires who stands no nonsense and gets on with the game, but in a friendly manner. He would ask me how my father was or what happened to John Reid, Bert Sutcliffe and other players of that era. He is not afraid to have a private conversation during play – even if it is something completely divorced from the action – just to give him a break. Otherwise, he will tell you whether you are bowling well or he might offer the theory that you will get a certain batsman out soon. 'Keep bowling there, he might nick one,' he would say to me. Dickie would smile as I beat the batsman again, as if he got a real thrill out of it.

Get a batsman out and his look would say, 'I told you so!' In a way, he motivated you. It is pertinent, too, that he is an umpire who has played first-class cricket.

Reproduced with permission from Rhythm and Swing *by Sir Richard Hadlee (MOA, NZ).*

5

CELEBRITIES

Richie Benaud never played with Dickie but wishes he did and Michael Parkinson, who opened the innings for Barnsley CC with Dickie, tells how his partner once got into such a twist he fastened his batting pads together so that when he stood up, he fell over.

Parkinson invented the phrase 'he could witter for England'. Former MCC secretary John Stephenson has some interesting revelations about Dickie's trip to Zimbabwe and TCCB chief executive Alan Smith describes him as 'a bit of an old fusspot'.

Richie Benaud
Doyen of cricket commentators and former Australian captain

———

Richie tells how Dickie nearly persuaded Dennis Lillee to become an offspin bowler.

I was unlucky. I toured England on three occasions and never met Dickie Bird on the field of play and it naturally follows that I also didn't have the experience of playing under him as an umpire. It was my loss because Dickie has been an outstanding umpire at international level, and he was a useful cricketer as well.

We almost played against one another in 1961 but there were two minor matters which stopped that: neither of us was chosen in the Leicestershire and Australian teams to play at Grace Road on 14 June. I had played at Edgbaston the previous day, the final day of the First Test, and my shoulder had given way and I had then travelled to London for treatment while Neil Harvey took the team to Grace Road. This was a good season for Leicestershire where they climbed eight places in the Championship and they were well led by Willie Watson who had a difficult time with selections. In the three games at that time, Leicestershire played Worcestershire, whom they thrashed at Coalville, went down to the Australians and then they demolished Northamptonshire at Kettering, all in the space of ten days.

Having missed the chance to try Dickie with a 'flipper', I at least had the good fortune to see all of his umpiring up to the time he started to flit around the world under the new National Grid scheme. I was there at Headingley when he made his umpiring début in 1973 in the England *v* New Zealand Test and I was there in 1975, the year of the first World Cup when the Headingley pitch was sabotaged. I'm glad Dickie wasn't standing in that game, it might have been too much for him. He was standing though at the Oval in the Fourth Test when Australia, after making 532–9, bowled out England for 191 and made them follow on.

It was just becoming fashionable for bowlers, if things weren't going well for them, to ask for the ball to be changed. On the fourth afternoon, in the course of the 151 match-saving stand between Woolmer and Knott, Dennis Lillee said to Dickie in mid-over that the ball was out of shape. Dickie said to Lillee that he should keep bowling and it might go back into shape. Dickie declined to change it, Lillee declined to bowl and that's why they both sat down on the ground at the pavilion end and looked at one another. Ian Chappell went over to find out what was going on, listened and told Dennis to get on with it, which he did, bowling offspinners.

After four immaculate dot balls to conclude the over, Dickie took the ball and went towards the spare umpire who was now coming from the pavilion with a box of balls. As he went past Dennis he said, straightfaced, to the greatest fast bowler in the world, 'You ought to think about a career as a slow bowler ...!'

Michael Parkinson
Former Barnsley opener

Dickie's former opening partner comes clean about the nervous habits which his friend has overcome to reach the top in umpiring.

To say Dickie Bird loves cricket doesn't get anywhere near describing what exactly he feels for the game. It is a bit like saying that Romeo had a slight crush on Juliet or Abelard had a fancy for Héloïse. The game consumes his life and defines its horizons. It shapes the very posture of the man.

Like a tree bent and moulded by the prevailing wind, so the curve in Bird's spine, the hunch of his shoulders, the crinkled eyes as he inspects the world, have been sculpted through a lifetime's dedication to cricket. He is, nowadays, one of the landmarks of the game – an umpire as famous as any superstar, as much respected by cricketers as he is loved by the public.

I have known him for forty years and he could have wittered for England when he was a teenager. He used to sit in the pavilion at Barnsley and chew his fingernails through his batting gloves while waiting for his turn at the wicket. On one occasion, and God knows how, he managed to fasten his batting pads together at the knees so that when it came to the moment he had to stride to the wicket he stood up and fell flat on his face.

I wondered if he was nervous before a game now. 'Terrible,' he said. 'In and out of the toilet. Can't stop wittering. But once I am on the field I change. I become calm and focused. I am never thrown by what happens out there.'

There have, however, been moments when he has been fazed. There was that time during a Test match when Allan Lamb walked into bat and handed Dickie his portable phone. 'What's this?' said Dickie. 'A phone,' said Allan. 'And what does tha' expect me to do wi' it?' he asked. 'Take calls,' said the player.

The prospect of a phone ringing in his pocket during a Test match triggered a few of Dickie's worry symptoms: the ruminative rub of the jaw, the shooting out of his arms in front of him in the manner of his great hero Tommy Cooper, 'Just like that, ahem.' The phone rang. 'Umpire Bird here,' said Dickie. 'Tell that bloody man Lamb to get a move on,' said Ian Botham.

Lamb has often been Bird's nemesis. At Old Trafford he removed all the wheels from the umpire's car and left it standing on bricks. On another occasion he locked the umpires' room from the outside and led his team on to the field leaving Dickie and his fellow official imprisoned. Play was held up while a steward with a sledgehammer knocked the door down, by which time Dickie Bird was a gibbering wreck.

I dwell on these anecdotes because he loves telling them and they give an insight into his formidable sense of humour. The man you see on television, the twitchy, careworn, fraught individual with head bowed against the troubles of the world, is only a part of the whole being. There is a lot of laughter in him. His cap is homage to Albert Modley, an old-time Northern music-hall comedian. He adores Tommy Cooper and Benny Hill. When he has a good laugh, like we did the other day, he sometimes cries with joy.

When Garfield Sobers appeared on Dickie's *This is Your Life* the umpire shed tears of happiness. 'Oh, master,' he said to Sobers. In all his years in the game, both as player and umpire, he has never lost his love for cricket's artistes. Who have been the players to move him to tears? Well, Sobers apart, there's Lillee – 'the greatest. That's all you can say – the best'; Barry Richards and Viv Richards; Boycott and Border – 'I'd have those two batting for my life any day'; Graeme Pollock, Greg Chappell, Michael Holding, Richard Hadlee. There are more.

'Fastest bowler I ever saw through the air was Frank Tyson. Lightning. Bowled against me at Scarborough and I went on the front foot and hit the first three balls through midwicket for four. As he bowled the fourth I was again on the front foot and all I remember was hearing him say "hit that bugger for four". Next thing I heard was the ambulance they sent to take me to hospital. I was trying to get up, saying, "Wheer's that

Tyson? I'll reighten him if I get hold of him!" ' He points to a dent in his jawline. 'Still feel it when it's cold,' he said.

He feels Wasim Akram, Waqar Younis, Curtly Ambrose and Malcolm Marshall are as good as any he has seen. Les Jackson comes close. 'Two Tests for England, it's a joke. If he played nowadays he'd be an automatic choice. Played against him once and he kept hitting me in t'ribcage. I went down t'wicket and said, "I wish tha'd stop bowling like that," and he said, "Why?" And I said, "Because I'm not bloody good enough to hit thi', that's why." '

When I asked him what gave him most satisfaction in life he said he thought it was that he thought his fellow professionals 'trusted' him. Interesting choice of word. Not 'loved' or 'admired' him but gave him their trust.

Reproduced with permission from Michael Parkinson.

John Stephenson
Former MCC secretary and President of the Forty Club

Mugged in Harare, the MCC come to Dickie's aid ... and Dickie comes to the aid of Zimbabwe by ending the drought.

In 1992 I represented the MCC at the inaugural Test in Zimbabwe when India were the opposition and Dickie was one of the umpires. As usual, Dickie arrived very early for his flight from London – midday when he didn't need to be there until 6 p.m. – and he arrived in Harare a day earlier than he needed to.

I went the next day and attended a meeting with the Zimbabwean officials and the ICC Match Referee Peter Van der Merwe to finalize the arrangements. Halfway through, Dickie suddenly burst in. 'Do you know, I've been mugged,' he said. 'I was walking in the street when this fella came up to me. He took £100. I might have been killed.'

We were naturally perturbed about it and offered our sympathy. 'But what am I going to do about the money?' he said. 'Surely you must be insured,' I said. He wasn't too certain whether he was covered.

After the meeting was over, I bumped into him again in the hotel and he recounted the story again. 'I've lost £200,' he said. The amount was going up by the hour. 'If you find you are not insured, I am sure the MCC will help you out,' I said.

Sure enough, when we all returned to England I heard from Dickie again, confirming that he hadn't been covered and I sent him a cheque ... for £100.

While on that trip to Harare I was having a drink with Jack Hampshire, the Zimbabwean coach and former Yorkshire batsman, and we were discussing Dickie's immense contribution to the game. 'I think he's the most popular figure in world cricket,' said Jack. 'I can't understand why he hasn't married.'

We talked about how marriage and a family might have changed him. Later Dickie joined us and we asked him why he had kept clear of the marriage vows. 'Came close in 1965 but I was always living in and out of a suitcase,' he said. 'It's too late now. I wouldn't think of it. Anyway, they've all got Aids these days.'

Jack put on a mild show of indignation. 'Are you saying my wife Judy has got Aids?' he said. 'Oh no,' said Dickie, 'not Judy. But you know what I mean.'

Next time I saw Dickie, I said, 'I hear you've been alleging my wife Karen has got Aids.' Dickie was quite agitated. 'No, no, not Karen,' he said. 'I didn't mean her. Not at all.'

Dickie would always come to my office at Lord's to see me when he was officiating there. He would knock at the door and say, 'Morning, Sir, what's the weather forecast. Have you heard?' I would usually try to pull his leg by replying, 'Not too clever, I hear. Rain is on the way.'

Once we had disposed of the awful prospect of what might happen if it did rain, he would change the subject and talk about his expenses. 'Don't forget my expenses,' he always said. 'I'm broke.' He is a personality and I know we say there aren't the personalities around these days but it is true. He is one of the last of the outstanding cricketing personalities, him and Ian Botham.

Roger Knight
MCC secretary and former Surrey,
Gloucestershire and Sussex batsman

———

Noisy ice-cream seller nearly stops play.

There was always a lot of fun when Dickie was in charge, more so when we were playing on an Essex ground. I remember one game where the Essex players were ribbing him about a noisy ice-cream man whom they claimed was putting them off. Dickie was so concerned he was about to leave the field to talk to the man when he realized it was a joke.

It is a great sadness to everyone that Dickie is now leaving the international arena but all good things must come to an end. He has been a wonderful ambassador for the game.

Sir Tim Rice
Lyricist and cricket lover

Tells of how easy it was to interview H. D. Bird.

I have two personal memories of Dickie Bird. The first was when he was a guest on my short-lived chat show on BBC2. He was by far the easiest guest I have ever had to interview as from the moment he sat down he launched into a string of reminiscences which continued unabated until his time was up. My one attempt at a supplementary question was greeted with the immortal words, 'I haven't finished my first answer yet.'

The other memory is when I asked him what he thought about the idea of neutral umpires. He admonished me sternly, saying, 'All umpires are always neutral – or should be.'

Peter Baxter
Producer of *Test Match Special*

———

Dickie is well wrapped up against the sun in Cambridge.

A glorious mid-April morning in Cambridge. The daffodils and pussy-willow were out, the sun was shining on Fenner's and how better to start the 1995 cricket season? Arriving early, the first person I saw was H. D. Bird. Today, I thought, he can have no worry about light or the firmness of the ground.

I gave him a hearty greeting, for having him launch the first-class season seemed entirely fitting. 'Oh, Peter,' he said with a frown, 'it's going to be cold. I've got seven layers to put on, seven layers I have.' I could vouch for the first six: a thick shirt, three cricket sweaters, a jacket and a white coat. The other one I had to take his word for. 'I've got me thermals on,' he said. 'Thermals ... oh, it's going to be cold.'

Dickie was a great favourite of John Arlott in his commentaries. The white peaked cap was always being mentioned by John. 'Dickie Bird – looking for all the world like a pantomime goose.' In the 1975 World Cup Final, Clive Lloyd was in full flow, destroying the Australian bowling, particularly that of Gary Gilmour. Arlott, too, was in full flow.

'Dickie Bird, having a wonderful time, signalling everything and stopping the traffic coming up behind, but he lets Gilmour in now ... ' We will cherish the memory of those furiously signalled fours. And I do hope he finds something good to worry about in retirement!

Alan Smith
Chief executive, TCCB

On Dickie as a correspondent.

Dickie has been a great ambassador for the game and his affection for it has always shone through. I do not know of anyone who is more enthusiastic, or more loyal to the game.

He is famous at Lord's for his letters. He will write every so often and always ends his letters 'thank you for your help and kindness'. It is a nice touch. After it was decided he would leave the Test panel in 1996 he wrote and said he agreed with the decision and it was in the best interests of the game that two younger umpires, Peter Willey and George Sharp, should be promoted.

I played against him and it never occurred to me that he would become an umpire. But he took to it so successfully that within three years he was voted on to the Test panel. He is very conscientious, almost to a fault. In the nicest possible way, he is a bit of an old fusspot!

117

Sir Garfield Sobers

Former West Indian captain and, in the opinion of many, the greatest all-round cricketer in the history of the game

---

Garry recalls the day when a couple of stiff brandies settled his stomach.

Dickie stood in the Lord's Test in 1973 which was my final one at the world's best-known cricket ground. My knee was giving me trouble at that time and I only played in the Test matches in that series.

Dickie stood in that match along with another umpire I had great respect for, Charlie Elliott. Along with the late Syd Buller, I put these two up alongside the Australian Col Egar as the best umpires of my time. It was well known that I liked to relax off the field over a few drinks and on the Friday night, when I was not out, I went out with an old buddy, Reg Scarlett. It was 5 a.m. before we returned to the hotel and even then I was unable to get any sleep.

Reg drove me to the ground and early on I played and missed a few times. Suddenly I felt churning pains in my stomach and felt like going off. As I was still about thirty runs short of a century I decided I had to continue. I didn't want to break my concentration.

But after I reached my hundred I said to Charlie Elliott, 'I'm not feeling well, can I go off?' Charlie was perplexed and so was Dickie. 'You're not injured,' said Charlie. 'What can I put it down to?'

'I can't stay,' I said. And off I went. In the dressing room the skipper, Rohan Kanhai, who always called me captain, said, 'What's the matter, captain?' 'It's my stomach,' I said. 'It's giving me trouble. I had to come off.'

Rohan turned to the twelfth man and said, 'Bring the captain a brandy and port to settle his stomach.' When it arrived, I soon downed it and Rohan said, 'Bring the captain another brandy and port.' That made me feel much better and when Keith Boyce was out, Rohan asked me to resume my innings.

118

As I came out, John Arlott, who was on air at the time, said, 'Goodness me, West Indies 604 for seven and here comes Sobers.' I can't remember what Dickie said but it was probably something witty because he always had a comment or two on these situations.

The West Indians love him because of his sense of humour and the way he talks to them. He is a real lovable man and I was honoured to be asked to take part in his *This is Your Life* programme. He was never shy of making the tough decisions and he made them decisively. He knows his cricket.

J. Paul Getty
Cricket's leading philanthropist

The owner of Wisden *has used Dickie's services at several of his charity matches.*

Dickie Bird is a phenomenon in sport. An umpire who is well known, and as loved, if not as well paid, as any of the glamorous stars whose antics he officiates.

One of the things that sets Dickie apart from the rest is his respect for conventions that for some of us are such an important part of our love for cricket. To see Dickie, tears welling in his eyes as he speaks of his MBE, reminds us of a better, more respectful time, even of long summer evenings of 'O my Hornby and my Barlow long ago'.

Dickie, very much true to form, is retiring at the right time. He is not the sort of man to need, or want, a third, square-eyed, umpire somewhere up in the stands.

Dickie will leave the public stage of cricket poorer, but he has established a criterion by which all future umpires will be judged. What a challenge to the upcoming generation!

You have to get up earlier when Dickie is on parade. We did a Test at the Oval once – I was again the third umpire – when we discussed what time we should leave on the morning of the first day. 'Better make it seven o'clock,' said Dickie. That was four hours before the start of play. 'Can't we make it seven forty-five?' I asked. I think we came up with a 7.20 compromise which left us with more than two hours to kill in the umpires' room. Usually Dickie sits there twiddling with his hair. It's amazing he's got such a full head of hair!

6

STARS FROM ABROAD ... AND OTHERS

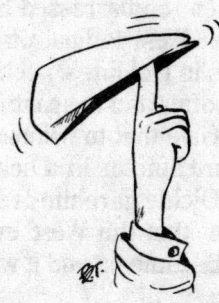

Brian Scovell recounts some of the more evocative stories about Dickie from admirers around the cricketing world.

The former West Indian fast bowler, Michael Holding, receives a £50 bonus from a West Indian fan at the Oval.

Dickie coined the phrase 'Whispering Death' to describe Michael's run up to the wicket. A former athlete in Jamaica, Michael would glide in with such elegance and stealth that umpires didn't hear him until he was past them.

At the Oval in 1976 when he took fourteen English wickets he was at his peak. It was a typical Oval pitch of the time – dry and lacking in pace. But Holding's accuracy and pace destroyed England as he made their skipper Tony Greig pay for his 'grovel' remark.*

The West Indies fast bowlers bowled faster and with more

* His comment 'We'll make them grovel,' was broadcast on television.

aggression whenever Greig came to the crease and the fielders looked more interested. Greig hit three fours off Holding in his first innings, all glorious drives through the offside field. But later in the same over, the tall, lithe Jamaican sent all three stumps flying into the air with a perfectly delivered yorker. Hundreds of West Indian supporters sitting on the Archbishop Tenison School side of the ground raced on and Dickie and fellow umpire Bill Alley were powerless to stop them trampling all over the pitch. The embarrassed Holding tried in vain to wave them away. One West Indian, obviously a rich man, tried to stuff some notes in Holding's pocket.

Holding declined the offer and the man approached Dickie. 'Here Dickie,' he said. 'Give that to Michael when you have a chance.' There were ten £5 notes in a neat roll. Holding was hoisted into the air and Dickie gave the order to leave the field once it became apparent that the West Indian fans were not going to go quietly. Police came on and it was thirteen minutes before play resumed.

The West Indies won the match by 231 runs and at the end of the game Greig came out to 'grovel' in front of the West Indian fans. Holding also dismissed him in the second innings. 'Finest exhibition of fast bowling I've seen,' said Dickie.

Greg Chappell, as captain of Australia, owns up in the shower.

One of the most frustrating moments for an umpire is when the batsman plays at the ball, appears to hit it but there is another sound which is not that of the ball making contact with wood. That happened to Dickie in the England *v* Australia series and the batsman was Greg Chappell in the Oval Test. Chris Old was the bowler and as he delivered an outswinger, Chappell played at it, jamming his bat into the ground as he did so and was caught. The noise of bat on ground drowned any other noise but Dickie was sure contact had been made and signalled out.

Afterwards he went to the Australian dressing room for a shower – in those days there were no separate facilities for the umpires – and came across Chappell. 'I thought I'd get away with that one,' Chappell said.

Australia's silent giant Graham McKenzie gave Dickie no problems.

One of Dickie's favourite Australian cricketers, with Dennis Lillee heading the list, was the Western Australian Graham McKenzie. Known as 'Garth' because of his physique, he was the only bowler Dickie ever came across who never appealed. 'He gave me no problems, none at all,' recalled Dickie. McKenzie used to leave it to his wicket-keeper and slips to do the appealing. Off the field, he was almost as quiet and gentlemanly.

Why Sarfraz Nawaz, former Pakistan and Northants bowler, never wanted to bowl at Dickie's end.

Sarfraz always had a set routine whenever he appeared in a match umpired by Dickie. He would see which end Dickie was standing and say to his captain, 'Captain, the other end please! This man is too good an umpire. No lbws from him!'

He used to call Dickie 'Dickie Dido' for some unexplained reason. In a Northants v Somerset match the Somerset quick bowler Allan Jones, now a first-class umpire, started bowling bouncers at Sarfraz, no mean feat because Sarfraz is six feet five inches tall. Sarfraz didn't mind but after one over full of short-pitched deliveries, he shouted down the pitch, 'Your turn will come. When you bat, I will knock your block off.'

'Now then, gentlemen,' said Dickie. Allan Jones got the message. Next over he bowled normally.

Another well-documented occasion when Dickie had to intervene and Sarfraz was the centre of attention was the Monday of the England v Pakistan Test at the Oval in 1974. Sarfraz's final ball before tea was a beamer, a head-high full toss and it was higher than a normal beamer because the batsman was Tony Greig, at six feet seven inches tall, possibly England's tallest ever player.

Greig was furious. He came striding down the pitch and said, 'I'm going to wrap this bat round your head.' Sarfraz, standing with his hands on his hips, said calmly, 'I am waiting for you.' Dickie promptly whipped the bails off and stepped in between them. 'That's tea, gentlemen,' he said. As the other players trooped off, he told Sarfraz and Greig to calm down. He told Sarfraz, 'I want no more of those beamers, please.' Sarfraz apologized and promised not to bowl another one.

Later Greig told Dickie, 'Thanks for the way you handled that situation. If I had hit him it would have been the end of my career.' Almost twenty years on, it is debatable how present-day umpires would have reacted. With slow motion TV, the extra publicity would no doubt have forced the authorities to take disciplinary action against both players.

Dickie offers some advice on a dodgy run to Keith Goodwin, former Lancashire wicket-keeper.

Keith was batting in a championship match against Hampshire at Southampton when he pushed the ball through midwicket and ran one. He looked up, called for a second and started off down the pitch only to hear a voice say, 'NO, Goody, no. Get back, there isn't a second.'

The voice was Dickie's, standing in one of his first senior matches. Keith failed to heed the advice and was run out for two. 'I got a bit carried away,' admitted Dickie.

How Gordon Greenidge and a West Indian runner confused Dickie at Trent Bridge.

Gordon Greenidge was opening for the West Indies against England in a Test at Trent Bridge when he strained a muscle and asked for a runner. The West Indies sent out Collis King and Tony Greig, the England captain at the time, promptly objected on the grounds that King, who was one of the fastest movers in the squad, wasn't included in the twelve named for the match.

Dickie ruled that anyone can run for an injured batsman. 'They could even send out the manager, Clyde Walcott,' he said. But after a delay while the matter was sorted out, the West Indies agreed to take King off and replace him with Larry Gomes. Section 5 of Law 2 merely says, 'the runner shall be a member of the batting side and shall, if possible, have already batted in that innings.' As Greenidge was an opener, that couldn't apply.

Greenidge was soon out and order was quickly restored. But when England batted, there was more confusion as a succession of substitute fielders came on and off. In the prevailing light, they all looked alike, someone said!

It turned out to be one of Dickie's more stressful Tests. The West Indies retaliated by protesting about a strapping on Chris Old's arm after he had been put in hospital by a delivery from Andy Roberts. 'It's putting us off,' they claimed. So Dickie had to tell Old to take it off if he wanted to continue bowling.

Bill Tidy

A short back and sides for the former India and Bombay opening batsman, Sunil Gavaskar, stops play at Lord's.

The first known instance of a haircut stopping play in a Test match took place at Lord's when Gavaskar complained that his hair was falling into his eyes and hampering his run-making. 'Have you got a pair of scissors, Mr Dickie?' he asked. He was surprised when Dickie produced a pair. Like all umpires, he invariably takes a pair out to the middle with him.

Dickie cut off the offending locks and Gavaskar said, 'I won't need to go to the barbers' again this summer!'

Later in the same series Tony Greig was standing so close on the offside when Gavaskar was batting that Dickie, concerned that the law on encroachment might have been breached, said to Gavaskar, 'Is that fellow bothering you? Is he fielding too close?'

Replied Gavaskar, 'Keep quiet, Dickie! He is fielding too close to catch me. It is a fielder wasted.' Greig had to continually jump out of the way when Gavaskar played attacking shots.

Dickie's calm intervention cools a heated situation at Edgbaston with Malcolm Marshall, the former West Indian, Barbadian and Natal fast bowler.

The England *v* West Indies series in 1984 saw a number of injuries to batsmen as the West Indian fast bowlers dug the ball in short. *Wisden* said 'batting against Marshall, Holding and Garner was as much an exercise in self-defence as protecting the wicket.' Andy Lloyd was put in hospital with a head injury and Paul Terry had his arm broken. The West Indies became the first touring side to win all five Tests in England but their reputation for fair play was dented.

Dickie Bird was the first umpire to step in and issue an official warning – in the Edgbaston Test when Lloyd was hurt – and the recipient was Malcolm Marshall. Because Ian Botham was batting at the time Marshall took exception and kicked the ball towards the boundary in anger. As Dickie called Clive Lloyd, the skipper, over he said to Marshall, 'Malcolm, while I am having a word with your captain I would like you to fetch the ball back.'

Marshall retrieved the ball and when he resumed bowling, pitched the ball up and was rewarded with a couple of wickets. Dickie also stood in the Fourth Test at Old Trafford and on arrival at the ground, bumped into Jackie Hendriks, the West Indian manager.

'By the way, Dickie,' said Hendriks, 'we're leaving Malcolm out because you are umpiring. We don't want him warned again!' But Marshall, who had broken a bone in his hand at Headingley, was unfit.

Not out off Denise Alderman's chest protector.

In 1982 Dickie was invited to umpire in the Women's World Cup in Australia which enabled him to become the first umpire to stand in a men's World Cup Final and also the comparable event in women's cricket. He spent six weeks in New Zealand and the highlight was his meeting with Sir Robert Muldoon, who was Prime Minister of New Zealand at the time.

In the England *v* Australia game Denise Alderman, the sister of former Australia and Kent opening bowler Terry Alderman, was batting when there was a loud appeal by the wicket-keeper and the close fielders for a catch behind. Not being certain whether the ball had caught the edge of the bat, Dickie said, 'Not out!'

When Denise got down to his end the next time, she said, 'That was a neat decision, Dickie. The ball hit my metal chest protector!'

The jostling incident at the Centenary Test at Lord's in 1980 when fellow umpire David Constant was nearly throttled.

One of the low points in Dickie's career came in the Centenary Test at Lord's in 1980 when he and fellow umpire David Constant were jostled by angry MCC members in the Long Room. Constant was seized by his tie and it was a frightening experience.

An hour's play was lost on the first day because of rain and almost two hours on the second day. That night it rained and just before play was due to resume on the Saturday, the skies cleared and it was a bright, sunny day. But part of the square on the Tavern side was still wet, not having been covered, and in regular inspections through the day the umpires ruled that it would be too risky to start. Umpires are always wary that a wrong decision could lead to a player being injured.

If the captains had been in agreement about resuming the match could have got started, but Ian Botham was in no hurry to play and it was left to the umpires. With the TCCB having no powers to intervene, it was a tricky situation for the organizers. As more alcohol was consumed, so the volume of noise, much of it hostile, increased. The umpires were barracked and, after their last inspection, molested as they made their way through the Long Room.

Former England captain, the late Peter May, who was about to take over as President of the MCC, found himself caught up in the controversy. On all sides he was being urged to tell the umpires to get on with it. Billy Griffith, the current MCC President and former long-serving secretary, could stand it no longer. He made his way to the umpires' room and told them they had to start ... and he would assume responsibility for what happened afterwards.

Peter May arrived a minute or two afterwards to give Griffith his backing and the decision was taken to recommence play immediately.

The day Bill Frindall, BBC Test Match Special scorer and statistician, 'gave' England an extra run!

Umpires have to wait for the official scorers to acknowledge their signals and sometimes confusion has arisen when a signal has been missed. This happened at Trent Bridge in 1976 when David Steele was caught at long leg by Andy Roberts off the bowling of Wayne Daniel and it was the seventh ball of the over.

Bill drew the attention of the *TMS* commentators to this fact and, interviewed by journalists later, Dickie admitted he had forgotten to signal a wide properly and see that it was acknowledged by the official scorers earlier in the over. He said he was too busy calling Clive Lloyd over to tell him Daniel was being warned for running into the prohibited zone and roughing up the pitch.

There was another occasion involving Dickie when a no-ball was missed by the official scorers. Dickie took Bill to the England dressing room after the close of play and announced the fact that the England total was being increased by one after an inquiry. Skipper Mike Brearley's announcement that Bill had scored his first run for England was greeted with loud applause from the team!

A confrontation between Shakoor Rana and an English gentleman and captain.

Pakistan's most infamous umpire had a few months umpiring in England in 1981 and Dickie stood with him in a match at Ilford when another English captain – not Mike Gatting – fell foul of him.

John Barclay, the Sussex captain who was assistant manager on recent England and England A tours, was bowling and Shakoor was in agitated conversation with him. Barclay had a puzzled expression on his face. 'I want you to come,' said Shakoor to Dickie. 'What's up?' said Dickie.

'I am giving the bowler a warning for running down the pitch and he does not agree with me,' said Shakoor.

'I am not running down the pitch,' insisted Barclay. 'Have a look and see if you can find any marks.' By now all the players were inspecting the disputed area and Dickie defused the situation by saying to Barclay, 'You've had an official warning, now let's get on with the game.'

Robin Jackman, the former Surrey and England bowler, was bowling to Gordon Greenidge, the former Hampshire and West Indies opening batsman and, unusually, he tried to bounce the man who was rated one of the finest hookers in the game. Greenidge went for the hook shot and the ball sailed high towards the square leg boundary. Dickie was standing on that side and in his excitement started running back as though he was the fielder and wanted to make a catch!

The ball dropped over the line with Dickie about twenty yards away shamefacedly signalling a six.

7

UMPIRES, SCORERS AND GROUNDSMEN

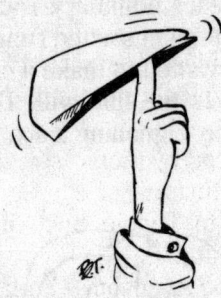

*Dickie's record of umpiring three World Cup Finals is unlikely
to be beaten, certainly not by an Englishman. When he retires,
scorers around the world will miss his idiosyncratic signals and
groundsmen will regret he is no longer there to be ribbed about
the impending heavy outbreaks of rain.*

David Shepherd
England's premier umpire and sole World Cup umpire

Shep recalls some painful moments for his illustrious partner.

I stood with Dickie at Headingley in 1988 when the incident of
the blocked drains held up play. Curtly Ambrose was bowling
and he stopped and said, 'I'm running in on water, it's up to
here.'

Dickie called me over and we inspected the scene. Water
was seeping up through the ground. 'We've got a problem

here,' said Dickie. 'What will we do?'

'Stick some sawdust on it,' I suggested. 'Sawdust?' he said. 'They'll need lorry loads of it.' The crowd couldn't understand what was happening and there was the usual calling out and booing which occurs on these occasions. The ground staff came out and started trying to soak it up and Dickie and I decided to take the players off the field.

As we left the field, one vociferous watcher shouted, 'You again, Bird. It happens every time you come here.' 'It's not my fault,' said Dickie. 'They need a plumber out there.'

After a delay, the problem was sorted out and the match resumed. It gave Dickie plenty to talk about for the next few days.

One of the dangers faced by umpires is that they can be hit, either by throws or a return hit or even by the bowler as he bowls. That happened to Dickie once in a Derbyshire *v* Hampshire game at Ilkeston.

The bowler was Keith Stevenson, who later changed clubs and joined Hampshire. Keith swung back his arm and caught Dickie under the chin. Dickie's knees buckled and he staggered around with the players holding him up. They naturally thought it was very funny.

When play resumed Stevenson bowled to Julian Shackleton, son of Derek Shackleton. There was a loud appeal for lbw and Dickie had enough of his senses about him to give him out.

I shall miss Dickie. We've stood together in some unusual places. Nagpur in India was one I remember. That is an experience I don't think I would want to repeat. His record of appearing in four World Cups, easily the best of the world's leading umpires, may never be beaten. He also umpired in three World Cup Finals and that is another record that will be hard to beat. I have stood in four World Cups now and was privileged to stand in the 1996 World Cup Final.

"I think Dickie is making another pitch inspection."

Ken Mahood

Jack Birkenshaw
Former Yorkshire, Leicestershire, Worcestershire and
England all-rounder and ex-umpire

---

*When it was three young lads in a bedroom at Leicester ... and
Dickie did some bed swapping.*

I was the first third umpire to be used when Dickie stood in
the First Cornhill Test against Pakistan at Old Trafford in
1987. Dickie and I were old friends right back to our days
together with Yorkshire and then Leicestershire. I kept saying
to him, 'Make sure you come off so I can take your place to
qualify for my £100 appearance money.'

'There's no way on earth I'm going to let you come on,' he
said. Anyway, Dickie was hit by a throw from Salim Malik and
went down in a heap. The physio went on and after looking at
the swelling on his leg, told him, 'I think you'd better go off for
a while, Dickie.'

Dickie wasn't having any of it. 'I'll not let that bugger come
on!' he said. It was pretty obvious though that he couldn't continue and they carried him off on a stretcher and I took over. I
got my money all right. But Dickie was soon back in action.

Another time I remember him having trouble was when we
went on a Swallows Cricket Club tour to the Far East, Australia
and New Zealand. There were so many flights and so many
stop-offs that it seemed the tour lasted months, not weeks. By
the time we eventually arrived in Sydney, Dickie's legs had
swelled up and he had to see a doctor. Told about our itinerary,
the doctor said, 'Whoever organized this trip for you is either
a genius, or a maniac.' We suspected the latter!

Most of the other players were professional people, lawyers,
accountants and that sort of person. We were jetting in and out
of so many countries that Dickie never seemed to have the
right currency. The others would volunteer to loan him some.
'Thanks very much,' he would say. 'I don't know about all this
money. Where are we?' I don't think he spent too much on the
trip!

My memories of Dickie and his habits go right back to the early Sixties when we were both on the staff at Leicestershire. There were a number of Yorkshiremen at Grace Road at the time and three of us, Dickie, myself and Bernard Cromack used to lodge with Geoff Burch in a council house. We had to sleep in the same room.

There wasn't a lot of space and Bernard used to sleep on a single bed and Dickie slept on a camp-bed on the floor which wasn't too comfortable. It might have been the start of his back trouble! Bernard had a girlfriend and would often come home late. Dickie would pinch his single bed and Bernard would wake him up to reclaim it.

Bernard then left the Leicestershire staff and took a job which meant he had to leave earlier in the mornings. Dickie got him to wake him up when he was going so he could take possession of the single bed. When you think about how Dickie lived in those days, it's a tribute to him that he got to the top of his profession and could stay in some of the best hotels in the world ... where he could sleep uninterrupted.

John Holder
First-class umpire and Test umpire

Dickie had more than his fair share of pitch invasions.

A few years ago Dickie was standing in a Second XI game at Old Trafford when the ball was hit hard along the ground in his direction at square leg, hit a divot and jumped up and caught him in the area which batsmen protect with their 'box'. Dickie doubled up in agony while everyone burst out laughing.

Sheena, Lancashire's lady physio, came on to provide first aid, ice pack in hand which Dickie declined at first, and advised him to go off for a rest. Later, he was lying on the treatment table when she came in to see how he was progressing.

'It's still swollen,' said Dickie. 'Three times its normal size! Is there anything you can give me to ease the pain while retaining the size?'

In 1986 he and Barrie Meyer had that amusing experience in the England *v* India Test at Edgbaston when two demonstrators, one male and one female, came on to demonstrate against something or other. The girl ran up to the stumps, removed the bails and stuffed them down her slacks. Dickie started to panic. Police officers came on and eventually a policewoman approached the girl and fished out the bails. Barry put them back in place, the police marched the couple off and we were ready to resume.

But not before Phil Edmonds went up to the wicket, took off a bail ... and held it to his nose to sniff. Dickie didn't know what to say.

He always had plenty to say about two particular bowlers, however. They were Arnie Sidebottom, the former Yorkshire and England bowler, and Paul Allott, the ex-Lancashire and England bowler who now commentates on the game for Sky. He called them 'the two gorillas'. 'They don't just appeal, they bellow at you,' he used to say.

The other funny experience Dickie was involved in which I

experienced myself came on a trip to Sharjah when we spent a relaxing hour or two at the seaside. Dickie was paddling about in about a couple of feet of water when he fell over. 'I'm drowning, I'm drowning,' he shouted. His arms were flailing around but it would have been difficult to drown in such shallow water. Nevertheless, we helped him up ... between the roars of laughter.

Dickie stood during another pitch invasion, at the Oval in the England v Australian Test. During a dull period of play, two men ran on and one lowered his trousers only to expose a bathing costume. He stood just off the Test strip while his mate went to the other end, marked out a short run and ran in to bowl a cheese roll down the wicket. After both men were escorted off, journalists asked the bowler if the cheese roll had turned when it pitched. 'The cheese turned but the roll went straight on,' he said.

I had many happy times with Birdie, as I called him, when we were in South Africa coaching together. There was one time when we were sent to a township and Dickie was more nervous than usual. 'I don't like the look of this,' he said. 'Let's go back to the hotel.'

None of the boys had arrived when we got there and we were debating what to do when scores of these little black lads in their smart school uniforms came round the corner. 'It's a Zulu uprising!' said Dickie.

They were quick learners and we had a great time with them. Dickie was a good coach, you know, he knew what he was talking about and could put it over in a simple way which youngsters could understand.

Peter Marron
Groundsman at Old Trafford

---

*In the Test when Peter took up his new job a forgetful Dickie said,
'... What we bloody need is a new groundsman.'*

I tell this story many times and it always raises a loud laugh. In
1983, the year I took over as Old Trafford groundsman,
Leicestershire were the visitors and the match was being
played right on the edge of the square. It wasn't a very good
pitch and the game was dying because the first day and a half
had been ruined by the weather.

Roger Tolchard declared Leicestershire's first innings 86
behind and had David Gower and James Whitaker bowling
long hops and full tosses as Graeme Fowler and Steve
O'Shaughnessy scored 201 in forty-three minutes, the fastest
double century on record. Steve's hundred took only thirty-
five minutes equalling Percy Fender's record for the fastest
hundred in first class cricket. It was the last match of the
season and as *Wisden* said, 'The season ended in travesty'.

As we came off, I was speaking to Dickie about the problems with the square and he said, 'If I were thee I'd go to
Cedric Rhoades [the then Lancashire chairman] and tell him
what we bloody need is a new groundsman!'

Nigel Plews, the other umpire, put a consoling arm round
me and led me away. Whenever I see Dickie now we always
have a laugh about it.

The B & Q incident in the 1995 Test between England and
the West Indies put Dickie on the front pages and we had a few
laughs about that afterwards as well. Since an old turnstile was
removed on that side of the ground there are a few occasions
in the summer when the sunlight reflects off the greenhouse
which is part of the B & Q store and play has to stop. It
happened a few years ago in a Test when David Gower was
batting.

This time the reflection was blinding and Dickie had no
alternative but to stop play while the groundstaff covered the

offending area with the black sightscreen which we use in Sunday matches. Then there was another hold up when the batsman complained about reflected light from the other end and Dickie, who was wearing two or three hats at the time, marched off towards the boxes to tell them to shut a window.

People in the boxes were winding him up. 'Give over Dickie,' said one. 'Come and have a drink.' It was a hot day and no doubt he felt like a drink.

He's got his mannerisms but he's been a great umpire and a lovely man. I'll miss my chats with him, particularly our recall of that comment he made back in 1983!

Umpires Harold Bird and Steve Bucknor leave the pavilion at Trent Bridge, first Cornhill Test, England *v* New Zealand, 1994.

Dickie in various moods:
expressive, contemplative,
thoughtful and communicative!

Umpire Bird awaits the third umpire's verdict at Old Trafford, fourth Cornhill Test, England *v* West Indies, 1995. The batsman, Mike Atherton, was adjudged run out.

(Left) Umpire Bird loses his cool when a glinting mirror interrupts play during the fourth Test at Old Trafford, England *v* West Indies, July 1995.

Dickie the showman.

Dickie's fairness, sense of humour and devotion to the game have defused many a tense situation on the cricket field; *(top)* congratulating New Zealand batsman Martin Crowe on a century against Somerset; and *(below)* warning Kenny Benjamin and Curtly Ambrose about their bowling, England *v* West Indies, June 1995.

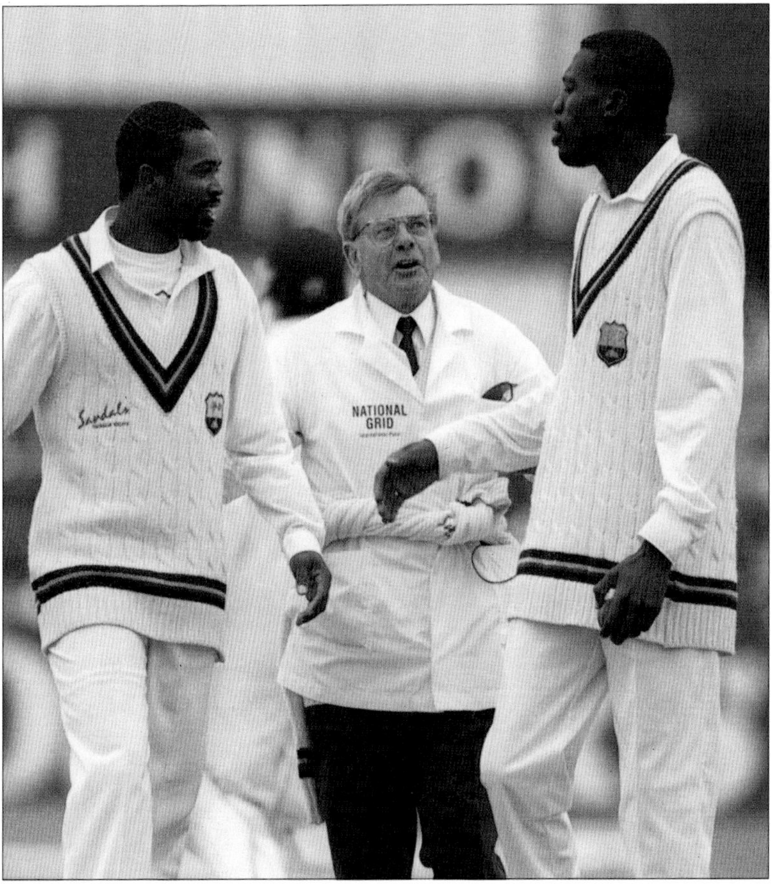

John Harris
Chairman of the First Class Umpires' Association

On the mystery of Dickie's missing blazer.

I will always remember Dickie for the drama of his missing blazer at Lord's. England were playing New Zealand and Her Majesty the Queen was due after lunch to be presented to the two sides. When we came off for lunch Dickie suddenly announced his blazer was missing. 'Someone has pinched it,' he said.

'Surely not,' I said. 'Only two of us have got the keys to the umpires' room.' 'No, it's gone, someone has taken it,' insisted Dickie. He called in Gareth, the security man. 'My blazer's been nicked, can you help me?' Dickie asked him. Gareth was too busy.

'I can't shake hands with the Queen without my blazer,' said Dickie. 'What do I do?' As I was the third umpire I suggested the solution might be to lend him mine. Dickie was very appreciative and the ceremonial duly took place with him wearing my blazer, which was a size too big for him. Afterwards he was still going on about it.

Later that night when we arrived back at the hotel he discovered his blazer was still hanging up in the wardrobe of his hotel bedroom!

Even funnier was an incident in a Kent *v* Surrey match at Canterbury when Chris Cowdrey, the Kent captain, complained about the state of the ball. After a lot of chuntering, Dickie finally agreed to a change and the groundsman Brian Fitch brought out a box of possible replacements. We started picking a few out and assessed them but Chris wasn't happy. 'They're too old,' he said.

There was one which looked the part but Dickie thought it was too new. There were also a couple which might have been serviceable but by this time balls were spilling out of the box and Dickie, becoming more agitated, was starting to throw some of them away.

The spectators were getting impatient and eventually we made a decision. Monte Lynch was the batsman and when the replacement ball was bowled at him he hit it straight out of the ground. It wasn't found and the pantomime had to start again. 'Where's that one that we thought might just be all right?' asked Chris.

'Dickie threw it away,' I said. I believe we did make a start ... eventually.

Mick Hunt
The head groundsman at Lord's

He's a good judge of a player ... and a streaker.

I've always called Dickie, Harold, and I think he likes that. When I first met him in the early Seventies and I was a member of the groundstaff I thought it was rude to call someone by a nickname so I called him Harold.

He will turn up the day before a Test at Lord's just to have a look around and see if everything is going like clockwork. One of his first questions will always be about the weather forecast. I usually have a stock answer. 'Awful, Harold,' I'll say. 'I've just been on to the Met Office and they say it's going to rain cats and dogs.'

'It's not?' he will say. 'That's not right, surely. Can't be. There's not a cloud in the sky.' Rain, interruptions, crowd noise ... they are all things we dread at a Test match. And especially bomb scares. I was there in 1973 when we had to clear the ground for more than an hour and a half.

Harold is a highly strung character as we all know but that day he was the coolest person around. In a crisis he always is. He was laughing and joking with the spectators. He was loving it. He's a showman, one of the few characters left in the game. After he goes there's only David Shepherd left and I don't know what will happen when he goes.

Harold was one of the umpires at Lord's in 1975 when that celebrated streak took place on one of the hottest days ever recorded in a Test match in England. It was 93 degrees and we were all feeling the heat when Michael Angelow, a twenty-four-year-old ship's clerk from St Albans, ran on and vaulted over the stumps to provide the newspapers with a front-page picture. Angelow said he did it for a £20 bet and when he appeared in court next day that was the amount he was fined. His mother said, 'I could see it was him on TV. I'll smack his behind when he gets home.'

Harold has always been very fair when marking up pitches.

The umpires have to report to the TCCB on Test pitches and if he has to mark one down he will come to me and tell me why he has done it.

He is also a very good judge of a player. We often chat and he will say, 'I've just seen a good 'un down at Hove.' Or somewhere. 'He'll go far in the game,' he will say. And usually he does. He doesn't get many wrong.

I feel for any batsman who scores a century in the 1996 Lord's Test against India because he will hardly get a mention. It will be Harold's Test.

Bill Tidy

Ted Lester
Former Yorkshire batsman and scorer

Was it a no-ball, or a wide?

During my long association with Yorkshire CCC one of my most pleasant duties was to award a Second Eleven cap to one H. D. Bird in my capacity as second-team captain. In 1958 Dickie suddenly emerged as a real challenger for a regular place in the first team but despite a number of appearances, including that innings of 181, he was not able to clinch a regular place and went to Leicestershire.

While he was with the second team we persuaded him to drink Guinness hoping it would build up his strength. Only he knows whether it worked. One lesson he has never forgotten from those days is that of punctuality. He often mentions how he arrives at various venues long before he needs to. Well, he was obliged to do this with Yorkshire otherwise he incurred a fine and being a true Yorkshireman he had no intention of paying one!

Never for one moment did I think this shy, nervous, excitable young cricketer could ever stand up to the pressures of umpiring, let alone become the number one in the world. I wondered whether he would spend as long in the toilet before going out to umpire as he did before going in to bat.

All scorers are told to accept and record the signals of umpires even though there may be occasions when the scorer believes the signals to be incorrect. There have been two identical occasions in my experience when Dickie has signalled 'no-ball' and then 'wide' from the same delivery.

This placed me in something of a predicament. Do I follow my instructions? I don't know whether the symbol is recognized, or simply record the no-ball? I have never previously mentioned this happening and maybe one day the administrators will agree that it is possible to have a wide from a no-ball, in which case Dickie was ahead of his time.

Many old ladies have wanted to mother him, in contrast to

many members of the public, particularly in Yorkshire, who have wanted to murder him when he has brought the players off the field for bad light or weather, or when he has delayed the resumption after a stoppage. I have to say that whatever his decision it has always been made with the interest of the players at heart and for that reason alone he has universal respect from all players.

It is sad to think that the day is not far away when scorers will not be awakened from their slumbers in mid-afternoon by the vociferous call of 'no-ball' or 'wide ball', when TV viewers will not be entertained by his eccentric mannerisms and when batsmen can 'pad up' knowing that any appeal will be carefully and fairly considered.

Alan Whitehead
First-class umpire and former Test umpire

The day the stumps were out of line and Dickie left them to it.

I was standing in a match between Lancashire and Derbyshire at Liverpool when Dickie called me over and said, 'I think there is something wrong at this end!' Bob Wincer, the Derbyshire pace bowler, had been bowling a lot of wides and I could see the stumps were set up in the wrong position. There was too much space on one side and not enough on the other.

'What are we going to do?' asked Dickie. I said I thought we ought to ask the captains to come out and discuss the matter. Bob Wincer wasn't too happy. He had bowled six no-balls and two wides and Barry Wood and David Lloyd, the Lancashire openers, were taking a lot of runs off him. Frank Hayes and Peter Kirsten were the two captains. There had been fifteen minutes play by the time we stopped the action.

After a few minutes discussion with them Dickie suddenly said, 'I will agree with whatever decision you come to, gentlemen,' and walked off! We agreed to abandon the game and start again with the stumps realigned in their proper position at that end. It ended in a high-scoring draw with David Lloyd, Barry Wood, Clive Lloyd and John Wright all scoring centuries.

Another amusing incident involving Dickie came in a Nottinghamshire match against the touring Indians. Before play started, Dickie said that Seb Coe was coming to see him. Seb was at the height of his powers in those days, a world-renowned athlete.

In a break during the first session I said to Dickie, 'You sure Seb is coming? I don't see him.' Dickie scanned the pavilion and the seats around it. 'Don't worry,' he said, 'he'll be here.'

At lunch there was still no sign of Seb. And during another break in the afternoon session I again asked Dickie whether his friend was really coming. 'He'll be here,' he said. 'Oh, really,' I said somewhat sceptically. Twenty minutes into the final session Dickie started looking agitated. 'He's here,' he announced triumphantly, pointing towards the pavilion.

'I don't see him,' I said. The seats were almost all taken. 'Fourth row back, left-hand side out in the front,' he said. Eventually I located the great athlete. After the close of play, Dickie introduced me to him and he was kind enough to sign autographs for my two young daughters. Dickie looked very pleased with himself. 'I suppose the next time we stand in a match together you'll say the Pope is coming to see you,' I said.

Not quite. Our next appearance together was in a Test at Lord's ... and it was Her Majesty the Queen. He's a great character is Dickie. I often think he should have been an actor, a character actor.

Brian Murgatroyd
Sky TV statistician

The last Bird of a somewhat undistinguished (except for him!) line?

Dickie Bird is the tenth member of the Bird clan to play first-class cricket. Sadly, none of them was particularly successful although Morice Carlos Bird, the former Lancashire and Surrey all-rounder, played ten Tests for England between 1909–13. He also went on MCC tours to South Africa, where his record was described as 'modest', and the Argentine. He scored 1,000 runs in a season on three occasions (to once by Dickie, in 1960) and captained Surrey just before the outbreak of the First World War. He died at the age of forty-five.

Most of the Birds played their cricket in the nineteenth century but an exception was the Warwickshire all-rounder Ronald Bird who scored 1,591 runs, average 37, in 1952.

Like Morice Bird, Austin Bird also played for Lancashire and Surrey. Born at Toxteth (can there be many Toxteth boys who made it to Lord's?) the two were brothers. Their father George (1849–1930) played thirteen matches for Middlesex and one for Lancashire for a career average of 14.45.

Albert Bird (1867–1927) played for both Warwickshire and Worcestershire, also unsuccessfully, and the Revd Frederick Bird, born at Framlingham, Suffolk, appeared for Gloucestershire and Northants around the turn of the century.

Percy John Bird (1877–1942) from West Cowes, in the Isle of Wight, managed one match for Hampshire and was the only Bird who kept wicket. Wilfrid Stanley Bird (1883–1915), a former Oxford Blue, played eleven matches for Middlesex before being killed in the First World War.

Walter Bird (1845–1921) played just one first-class match, for the MCC in 1880. Harold Dennis Bird, the only Yorkshireman, was the only one to go on and become a first-class umpire. Dickie bowled medium pace and his career bowling figures were 0–22. He also took 28 catches in 93 matches.

Chris Balderstone
Former Yorkshire batsman and first-class umpire

Baldy recalls standing with Dickie.

Many of my funniest moments since I became an umpire in 1988 have happened when standing with Dickie. He's always had sinus trouble, or says he has. A few years ago we were doing a Second XI match at Collingham and it was right in the middle of the hay-making season. He kept complaining about the discomfort and at lunch he suddenly produced a mask which he said he was going to wear.

The groundsman at Collingham is a bit of a character who goes home for lunch. When play resumed in the afternoon session the groundsman returned, saw Dickie out in the middle wearing this mask and shouted, 'We know it's you, Dickie! You can't fool us!'

I was the third umpire when he had all those problems with the reflection of the sun at Old Trafford in 1995. Most umpires would have let the groundstaff deal with it but Dickie being Dickie he marched over to the part of the ground where the glare was coming from, arms waving and shouting, and when he reached the advertising boards he tripped over and nearly went headlong. 'I nearly had you on, Baldy lad,' he said. 'Nearly sent for you!'

Another time we were together at Old Trafford for an opening game of the season. I arrived full of enthusiasm only to see Dickie hunched in a corner seat in the umpires' room. 'I'll be bloody glad when it's all over, Baldy lad,' he said. 'It gets harder, tha' knows.'

8

FROM THE PRESS BOX

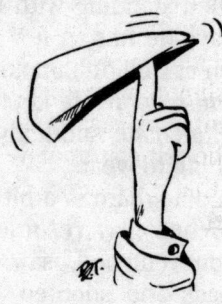

Dickie has always had a good relationship with those who wrote about cricket and here some of the game's finest writers give their verdict.

E. W. (Jim) Swanton
Doyen of cricket writers and commentators

Dickie was up with Frank Chester says the man who knew them both.

When I think of umpires the name of Frank Chester springs at once to mind. Starting young because of a First World War wound, Frank was outstanding, lifting the status of his vocation by dint of his personality, coupled with the excellence of his judgement.

To write of Dickie Bird in the same breath is a high

compliment which I believe is not undeserved. When both were in their prime a mistake was a rarity and they therefore enjoyed the confidence of the players. They had both also been cricketers of account, and accordingly were able to identify with them in a way which was scarcely open to those who, for all their qualities, have not themselves been through the mill.

In these days, when the spotlight beats so fiercely upon all concerned out in the middle, a bond of fellowship between the umpires and players is an ideal both parties should struggle hard to preserve.

It is sad that Dickie should have decided not to submit himself any more to the trauma of Test cricket; so let us be thankful for the rare dedication and humanity he has shown over many years, and hope that in the county game he may serve for further summers yet.

Martin Johnson
The *Daily Telegraph*

A few days after Dickie announced his retirement from Tests,
Martin spent a day with him.

We met for lunch in his favourite restaurant near Barnsley –
'You can have as much on your plate as you want here you
know' – and the car park was shrouded in fog. 'Where's the
light meter? There'll be no play before lunch,' he chortled.

I thought he looked a bit tired. 'Aye, woke up at four o'clock.
Terrible dream. It were those boogers Wasim and Waqar
appealing for lbws again,' he said. 'Did you give any?' I
enquired. 'Nay, "Not out! Not out!" I were shouting.'

Anyone inside hoping for a quiet meal was out of luck. The
world's most famous cricket umpire was in irrepressible form
and his voice carried all the way to Rotherham never mind the
next table. For some reason, a diner came over and started
telling us about his recent heart attack. 'It's amazin'. I've
niever 'ad one,' said Dickie.

'I could worry and witter for England, me,' said the man who
invariably introduces himself with, 'Pleased to meet you.
Harold Dennis Bird. Dickie to my friends.' As he hasn't an
enemy in the world, no-one calls him anything but Dickie.

He said, 'I were listening to radio from South Africa t'other
day and Ian Botham paid me a lovely compliment. He said I
was the best umpire who ever lived. Tremendous that. Ian said
I were honest, I were fair and I were consistent. That's what he
said. He also said I were bonkers.'

All this was spoken with one arm pinning my eating hand to
the plate and the familiarly manic delivery style which suggests
that the information he is imparting is beyond human compre-
hension. 'D'yer know? D'yer know what? This is true, this is ...'
is how he normally opens a topic of conversation and just when
you think he is about to reveal something that will shake the
cricket world to its foundations, he is just as likely to say, 'D'yer
know? D'yer know what? I had two poached eggs for me

breakfast. I did. Aye. It's true is that.'

On the field, he hunches over the bowling stumps with the screwed-up grimace of a man who is sitting on the wrong end of a shooting stick with a couple of thousand volts running through it, by the way he constantly jerks out his arms. Every now and again, albeit not often enough as far as bowlers are concerned, one of his arms shoots vertically above his head.

'That's out! That's out!' he cries, almost tearfully, as though he has just sentenced someone to death rather than a return trip to the pavilion. Most of all, though, he worries about everything and anything and is rarely without that 'why does it always happen to me?' expression.

He has made a career out of peering at the sky, although once, when water began gushing up his trouser leg from a burst drain at Headingley, trouble came from the opposite direction. He has ended a five-year drought in Sharjah by the simple expedient of putting three stumps into the ground and calling 'play' and he has also brought the teams off the field for, would you believe, an excess of sun in Manchester. But after the final day of the Lord's Test against India on 24 June, 1996, Harold Dennis Bird will retire from the international stage at the age of sixty-three.

He is already worrying – not least, being an emotional man – about how many boxes of tissues he will need. If play is held up while the groundstaff are chucking sawdust on the umpire's tears, it will be the ultimate entry in Dickie's 'It always happens to me' ledger.

'I'm praying already,' he says. 'Dear Lord, no rain please, no bad light. Not for this game, dear Lord. I've been out in Australia umpiring the series against Pakistan, and the first morning of the first game at Hobart, there is a close run out. So I call for the TV. I wait for the lights to go on, but nothing happens. They've broken down. Oh Christ, not me agin, I think. They come on the walkie-talkie. "Sorry Dickie, we've had a breakdown. You will have to do it yourself." Always happens to me.

'It's like that time we had the blocked drain at Leeds. I said to Shep "We've got a problem." He says, "Stick some sawdust down Dickie." I say "Sawdust? We'll need three lorry loads."

So off we come and I know I'm for it. There's this bloke screaming, "You again, Bird. Every bloody time you come here." So I said to him, "What d'yer mean me again? It's like a boating pond out there. I'm an umpire, not a bloody plumber." '

He has no doubts he is going at the right time – 'It's a younger man's job nowadays' – although he denies the suggestion that it is television's increasing intrusion into what was once a job for humans which has hastened his decision two years ahead of compulsory retirement age.

Bird is not comfortable with machines, as anyone who has heard his telephone answering machine – it sounds like a Dalek with a Yorkshire accent reading from a cue card – will know, but he says, 'I'm in favour of TV replays and the third umpire. Just as long as they don't start using them for lbws and such like.'

Bird made his name turning down lbw appeals. Early on in his umpiring career, he attended a Yorkshire practice and asked the players to bowl at a set of stumps. 'D'yer know, d'yer know ...' he said, 'd'yer know how long I stood there. Twenty minutes. I said, "gentlemen, please, will someone please hit these stumps so I can go home." Look at these shoot-outs they have in Cup games. Nobody can hit t'bloody wicket. Yer see, it's all about angles.'

Bird's lasting legacy, particularly in the modern hard-nosed era of sledging, pressured appealing and non-walking, is the fact that no other umpire earned such unqualified respect from players from every cricketing nation.

Even in Pakistan, where English umpires are generally regarded as strong candidates for a fatwa, Bird is regarded as the best there has ever been. This is partly due to his decision-making, but mostly down to the curious fact that Dickie in one of his flaps has a curiously calming influence on the most heated situation.

When a fielder claims what Bird feels is a dubious catch, or there is some dispute as to whether a ball has gone over the boundary or not, it is not unusual to see Dickie sprinting across to conduct his own investigation. 'I'll go up to 'em, look 'em in the eye and say, "Look, I'm here now and I want you to be honest. If you lie to me," I'll say, "the good Lord will send you straight to hell." I remember Merv Hughes swearing at Graeme Hick in a Test at Headingley and I went up to him and I said, "Mervyn, Mervyn, goodness me. Why are you swearing at that man? What harm has Mr Hick ever done you? Mervyn, your language is terrible. Terrible." And Mervyn looked at me and said, "Dickie, you're a legend."

'He's got a chat show on the radio in Australia now. Invited me on it last time I was in Melbourne. Lovely lad off the field. He's a character, too. Not many of those around any more. That Dennis Lillee, he put a rubber snake in me pocket. In a Test, too. Would that happen today? Would it bloody hell.'

Dickie never got married – 'married to cricket' – and his sister comes in to cook and clean for him. He lives in the South Yorkshire mining village of Staincross, about a mile from Geoffrey Boycott. 'Huge place he's got, but I've got better views over the Pennines. He invited me round to lunch once, but I didn't get any answer from those machines he's got on his front gate and had to climb over the wall. Toasted cheese sandwich was what I got. Then I was in Delhi once, and he said, "Dickie, I'm going to take you to dinner." I said, "Hang on a minute while I lie down."

'"Why do you want to lie down?" he said. I said, "Because you're the biggest miser I've met in my life. You'll put all your money in your coffin when you go, and I hope I am still around when they bury you, 'cos I'll be right over the graveyard to dig it up." Anyway, off I went to meet him for dinner in the hotel foyer, and he gave me two bars of fruit and nut, and said, "Have a nice dinner, Dickie" and off he went.

'If I had to pick a man to bat for my life it would be Boycott, but he'd want to know how much it was worth before he took guard.'

The happiest day of his life, he says, was when he was invited to lunch with the Queen – 'got more than a toasted sandwich' – and the saddest will undoubtedly be when he leaves the Test arena for the last time at his beloved Lord's. By the end of the 1997 summer, he will have to retire from the first-class game as well, so what will he do with himself?

He said, 'Travel all over the world watching cricket and

spending my money. D'yer know? D'yer know? If I plonk myself into a chair and sit in front of the telly, I'll be dead inside twelve months. The good Lord will look down and say, "What 'yer doing in that chair, Bird? I'm givin' thee out, Bird. That's out." '

Reproduced with permission from the Daily Telegraph.

David Foot
Author and freelance journalist

How Dickie boosted the confidence of 'Syd' Lawrence ... and others.

Most of the players seemed to agree on one thing: Dickie could be both infuriating and immensely likeable and warm-hearted. Often more or less at the same time. Some of his stories at the bar could go on a bit ...

He had a most generous side. When David 'Syd' Lawrence first arrived on the scene in Bristol his bowling was all over the place. Dickie pondered on the problem the raw fast bowler had with no-balls and running on the wicket and, on the Sunday morning, quietly took him aside and explained where he was going wrong.

As for Dickie's oddball humour, you have only to ask a succession of bowlers. One recalled, 'He was apt to call me the best slow bowler in the country and he just couldn't understand it ... as my ball landed in the River Tone at Taunton.'

Henry Blofield
Broadcaster and writer

Dickie couldn't take the air-conditioning out there with him.

Cricket is about the only sport that would produce a character like Dickie. Everyone loves him and you cannot say that about too many people. He has always been very friendly to me. 'What do you think, Henry?' he'll say, and then proceed to ignore what I've said and go on talking himself.

His greatest quality, I feel, is that he has been able to cope with the difficult players and not upset them. He has humoured them ... but still controlled them and got them playing the game in the right way.

One of my favourite stories about him is about a spat he had with an Australian bowler in a Test at Lord's. After Dickie turned down his appeal, the bowler was so upset that he said, 'You're an (expletive) Dickie!' Dickie looked at him and said, 'Aye, that's what my father always called me.'

I was with him in India in 1987 for the World Cup and I saw a lot of him with his fellow English umpire David Shepherd. Shep would walk around the streets acclimatizing himself to the heat and the conditions whereas Dickie spent most of his time in his air-conditioned room. 'Great hotel this, Henry,' he said. But when they went out to umpire Dickie found he couldn't take the air-conditioning with him and had a few problems. He was a bit fraught for a while.

He never did see CMJ bat.

The only time I played in a match officiated by Dickie Bird he fell ill with sunstroke before I got to the wicket. The match was in Dubai, in the searing heat of the Persian Gulf, and I was greatly disappointed, especially as I made a few runs. Vainly, I had wanted to impress upon this deepest of cricketing devotees that I could play the game a bit. I actually craved a couple of muttered asides in that deep, growling Yorkshire voice, 'Good shot mate' or 'You timed that one, Chris.'

All in the imagination, alas, but it is always like that when an amateur finds himself performing in the presence of a great professional; and there has been no better pro in his chosen field than Harold Dennis Bird. With Frank Chester and, in a shorter career, Syd Buller, he contests the right to be called the best umpire who ever lifted a finger, although in this toughest of all the jobs on the cricket field comparisons are perhaps particularly odious.

What he has achieved, above all, is an increased respect and affection for his profession. Umpires, like wicket-keepers, are supposed to be unobtrusive. Dickie has managed to be in the centre of the picture to everyone's greater pleasure, yet never at the expense of doing his job. With a magical balance he has contrived on one hand to be a character, a comic and an entertainer and on the other an absolutely impartial and dedicated arbiter, as near to flawless in his decision-making as it is possible for a human to be.

The more his job has been trespassed upon by machines in the last few years, the more one has questioned the wisdom of taking away one jot of the umpires' control of the game. In theory the use of the video replay to prove either way whether a batsman has been stumped or run out has saved the umpire from getting such decisions embarrassingly wrong. In practice, for various reasons, it has merely humiliated umpires further. I suspect that the first thoughts of retirement from 'big-match' cricket occurred to Dickie in 1995 when in one match he failed to call for a replay when he should have done and then in another a few weeks later found himself ridiculed by the crowd for summoning the third umpire, just in case, when everybody could see that the batsman had been out by miles.

Although he fretted and muttered and wondered why bad weather always seemed to follow him on big occasions, Dickie could take punishment from the crowd when it came to decisions about bad light or rain; but not about one of his precious decisions. He is, after all, a perfectionist and when that damned, pervasive slow-motion camera showed that he had reprieved Dermot Reeve in the NatWest final when he should surely have lifted the finger to declare him as plumb leg-before as anyone ever has been, he wisely decided to quit whilst he was ahead. Miles ahead, indeed. All the best Test players of his era agree that he was the best: warm-hearted, fun to play with and, ninety-nine times out of a hundred, dead right.

The other great paradox about him of course is that he has always been a bag of nerves, both on and off the field, yet when it comes to making a decision in the heat of the fiercest battle an icy coolness comes upon him and he is able to see, with impeccable clarity, which way he should answer an appeal.

You only have to discuss cricket or cricketers with Dickie to appreciate how indecisive he can be. 'Who do you think should open for England with Mike Atherton this season!' you might ask him over a beer at the end of an early-season county match.

'Alec Stewart, Chris, no question. Class batsman. There's no substitute for class, Chris.'

'But don't you think we need a left-hander, Dickie. Nick Knight perhaps?'

'Good player, Chris. Nick Knight. Good player. He's got heart. There's no substitute for heart. Left-hander, too. Left-hand/right-hand combinations. They're always the best. Mucks up the bowler's line. He'll be good, Chris, Knight. Mark my words.'

'How do you rate Jason Gallian?'

'Good technique, Chris. Best technique in the country. Big innings man. That's what we need. Once he's in he doesn't give it away, Gallian. That's what we need. Alec gets himself out too often when he's got to thirty. He's a number three is Stewart. A number three.'

Whichever one the actual selectors go for, however, will know he is in good hands when Javagal Srinath raps him on the pads apparently in line with the stumps from the Pavilion End at Lord's and leaps in appeal with arms upraised and brown eyes flashing. In an instant the line and height of the ball, the degree of the slope and the exact point at which the pad was struck will be weighed quickly and correctly. 'Not out!' Dickie will say, as likely as not, and as the disappointed bowler comes past him he will hear 'Just too high, mate. Going over. Well bowled, though.' And because it is Dickie, the bowler will accept the verdict with a smile.

The white cap, the booming voice, the little accidents, the anxious peer beneath hunched shoulders, the nervous shooting of hands and wrists from the sleeves of his white coat; the sheer fun he conveyed far beyond the 22 yards he controlled, over the boundary, into the crowd, even into the television rooms of a million homes: how we will all miss him when the 1996 Lord's Test has passed into history with all the others.

Don Mosey
Formerly of *Test Match Special*

After a few hundred anxious telephone calls, it was his life!

It all seemed very simple and straightforward. All I had to do was ask Dickie to join me in the studios of Yorkshire TV in Leeds to record a programme of cricket chat. And they would do the rest. 'They' were the independent TV company which at the time produced *This is Your Life*. And it has to be said that they were as good as their word. Everything else was taken in hand. Periodical reports reached me of the progress of the preparations. It was all going very smoothly.

What had not been anticipated, and certainly should have been, especially by me, was the fact that Dickie is never happier than when he has something to be unhappy about. It was early in the year when I first contacted him and the programme was to be recorded in September. Where Dickie is concerned, it is a long time from January to September. He had all the scope he needed to worry himself into a positive frenzy. He responded to my first contact, bless him, by agreeing at once. Certainly he would be glad to join me and talk about cricket before the TV cameras. I reported to London that all was well.

Within forty-eight hours he was on the phone again. 'What would we be talking about?' he asked. Well, that wasn't too difficult to sort out. We had known each other for a long time. 'There will be no shortage of subject matter,' I said. 'I've always found these things go better when they are spontaneous. This is no time to concern ourselves with what we're going to say. It'll be quite painless and I'm sure we'll enjoy ourselves.

'There will be an audience of Yorkshiremen and women who will simply be looking forward to hearing a lot of cricketing yarns. There's no shortage of them, is there?'

Dickie agreed. 'What time do we start?' he said. I said that as we would be recording about five thirty, four o'clock would be a good time to meet. All was well. A week later he called again. Did I think 4 p.m. would be early enough? I did. It was. A fortnight went by and I began to think that Dickie was at last easier in his mind about the operation, still seven and a half months away. Foolish fellow that I am. The phone rang. Was I absolutely certain 4 p.m. was the right time to meet? Yes, old friend, I am absolutely sure.

Another week passed before the next call. Could I give him some idea of the topics to be discussed? With a bit of quick thinking which surprised me I offered three or four ideas. They, in turn, brought six or seven supplementary queries. I thought I had managed to resolve most of his doubts and fears. Before he rang off, he asked, 'Surely we ought to meet before 4 p.m?' With an alarming picture before my eyes of Dickie rolling up to the studios at the same time as busloads and carloads of people he had known all his life, I swore solemn oaths that 4 p.m. would be absolutely and positively fine.

March was now approaching. There were two more calls before the cricket season began and I felt comfortable that with Dickie once more on the Test and county circuit his mind would be focused firmly on adjudication and not on the forthcoming (five more months) TV programme. Foolish fellow that I am!

It was a busy summer answering the phone to him. As September approached, and my, how slowly those months passed, his calls became progressively more agitated. By the end of the cricket season he was more of a gibbering wreck than he has ever been in the most dodgy 'bad light' situation and his phone bill must have been reaching the level of the Mexican national debt. At last, September arrived. Dickie made one last effort to have the meeting time brought forward by at least an hour. On the strict instructions of the programme producer in London I stoutly resisted. Four o'clock would be just fine. We would then have an hour, at least, to discuss what we were going to discuss. Absolutely no need to worry about anything.

Nevertheless I could hear faint alarm bells ringing as I drove the 85 miles from my home to Leeds on the afternoon of the recording. They became louder every mile I travelled. To be doubly safe, I timed my arrival for 3 p.m. I rushed into reception and enquired, with only the faintest touch of hysteria, 'Mr Bird hasn't arrived yet, has he?' It was more of a plea than an enquiry. A commissionaire, overhearing the question, turned to me and said, 'Thank goodness you're here. Mr Bird came at 2 p.m. and I've been going mad trying to keep him out of sight for the past hour.'

I joined Dickie in the small room where he had been going through various stages of claustrophobia for the past sixty to seventy minutes and where he had to remain incarcerated for at least another hour and a half. Edgar Allan Poe would probably be the best man to describe the period that followed.

At last a knock on the door announced that the studio was ready for us and there has never been more welcome news in my entire life. But the drama still had a little way to run. We were ushered into a studio set up with props of a cricket pitch with a set of stumps and two chairs and waiting there was a pretty large audience all expecting to hear half an hour of cricketing anecdotes. With a dry mouth and every nerve in my body jangling, I opened, 'Let's start with the story of Ian Botham, Allan Lamb and the mobile telephone, Dickie.' And away he went, marvellous raconteur that he is in his unique style. We were nearly there. Next question, 'Tell me, what's the most awkward situation you have encountered in your career?'

Dickie paused, gulped, drew a deep breath. This hadn't been mentioned to him in the stuffy little room backstage. What was going on? 'Well,' he said. 'Er, awkward moments, eh? The most awkward moment, er, well, EE Don, that IS a bit, er ...'

And Michael Aspel, red book in hand, ghosted gently out from behind a curtain. Never in my life have I been so glad to see anyone.

On a devoted man who lives for cricket.

Harold Dennis Bird, known thereafter as Dickie Bird, is exactly as you would expect him to be. He is caring and highly strung; he counts his blessings and lives for cricket; he has never been married and is a bit of a card.

His greatest sadness was never to be awarded his county cap for Yorkshire. He did win one for Leicestershire but earning a living as a county professional was always something of a struggle for him.

Cricket is a game that is in people's bones. Some who may not themselves be great exponents of it, understand it by instinct. Others, although they might be outstandingly effective as players, hardly know the first thing about it. There have been England captains who have been blind to many of its possibilities. Dickie, for his part, has a good feel for cricket. This, together with a disarming personality and a complete lack of arrogance, accounts for his success.

He drinks very little, never smokes and does his exercises every morning in the bathroom. If he wanted to, he could go on umpiring in first-class cricket until he is seventy and he will be quite lost without it. Alec Skelding, another umpiring character of his time, was seventy-two when he packed in. More recently, John Langridge was seventy. Umpiring is both Dickie's hobby and his livelihood. He goes all over the world doing it.

At Bulawayo he beat Frank Chester's record number of Test matches. Chester had been a batsman of high promise for Worcestershire before being badly wounded in the Great War. He umpired his first Test match, with trilby hat and artificial hand, at Lord's in 1924 and his forty-seventh and last at Lord's in 1955.

The fastest bowler 'through the air' that Dickie has umpired was Frank Tyson, the best was Dennis Lillee, the most prodigal appealer was Abdul Qadir and the cricketer he had most fun with was Allan Lamb.

Dickie lives, as the crow flies, a mile from Château Boycott in Barnsley. 'Aye,' he jokes, 'the rich man in his castle and the poor man at his gate.' Dickie was Barnsley's star batsman when Geoffrey Boycott first played for them as a boy. Before opening the innings Bird, hands shaking, would go to Boycott and say, 'Put me gloves on for me, will you, Gerald?' To this day Dickie calls Boycott 'Gerald' and 'Gerald' believes that then, as now, Dickie puts his nervous energy to advantage. 'He likes people to think he is an easy touch,' Boycott says, 'but he's not. Deep down he's quite strong and very fair.'

A man of humble tastes and honest opinions, tempering justice with mercy, presiding at great cricket events, a born worrier yet happy in his work – that is Dickie Bird, and if you ask him to your cricket dinner he'll give you good value there as well.

David Warner
Bradford Telegraph and Argus

Tea twice over at Perth.

Yorkshire's team of 1984 will long remember their trip to Scotland when Dickie was involved in what became known as 'The Case of the Two Tea Intervals'. It is rare for Yorkshire to travel anywhere by coach but one was laid on for the journey from Leeds to Perth where they were due to meet Scotland in a Benson and Hedges Cup tie the following day.

Usually, the players are happier travelling by car but were only too glad to sit back and relax on this occasion because it was after six-thirty when Yorkshire finally beat Somerset by six runs at Headingley in an exhausting BAC game. Dickie and John Holder, the umpires at Headingley, were also in charge of the Perth game and they, too, were among the party which at last trundled north on what must have been one of the slowest coaches ever to make the trip across the Border.

Dusk turned to black darkness and it was nearer to dawn than midnight when the bus drew up alongside the team's hotel. Suddenly there was a cry of alarm from Dickie who had just been told that Inverness was not next door to Perth and that he would not be able to make a local call to a friend for an overnight stay. He was mortified at having to stump up the cash for an expensive hotel room but was short on options. The alternative was a few hours kip under the covers at the North Inch ground.

Next day dawned bright and Dickie's troubles seemed far behind him as the game moved steadily on, Scotland's reply to Yorkshire's 231–7 being 25 overs old when the teams came off for tea. Dickie was just disappearing into a marquee when mutterings reached his ears that tea should have been taken after 35 overs, not 25 and he and John Holder had brought them off too early.

'It's twenty-five overs, *twenty-five*, it's always been *twenty-five*,' he told everyone in earshot and beyond. He was then

173

confronted by the secretary of the Scottish Cricket Union with an official letter from Lord's showing that the tea interval rules had indeed been changed and that the break now came after 35 overs. Neither Dickie nor John had received notification from Lord's and Dickie was considering what action to take when an old man of about eighty-five came up, tugged him by the sleeve and said, 'Mr Bird, I have umpired in local league cricket for well over sixty years and life would not be complete without meeting the greatest umpire in the world.' To the old man's surprise, Dickie's response was to bawl in his ear, 'What should I do? What should I do?'

In the event, Dickie decided to hold another tea interval ten overs later, just to make it all official and when he eventually got home to Barnsley he found the Lord's edict lying on his mat.

On the trip home, he showed he could display the wisdom of Solomon off the field as well as on it. The skipper Phil Carrick was going up the coach collecting for the driver but when he got to Geoff Boycott's seat he found the great man fast asleep.

Needing someone else to chip in for Boycott, he turned to Dickie and said, 'Throw a quid in for Boycs.' 'Don't be daft,' exploded Dickie. 'I'm not doing that. I'll nivver get it back. Nivver. I won't see that pound again. *Nivver*!'

Alex once nearly ruined Dickie's supper and still regrets it.

If you are an umpire and your name is Dickie Bird with a worldwide reputation to defend it cannot be pleasant to be told in the middle of a meal that a visiting Test captain has charged England's batsmen with deliberately running down the pitch to roughen those parts their spin bowlers might exploit in due course.

I still regret that I might have spoilt Dickie's Barnsley chop that evening during the England *v* Pakistan Test at Edgbaston in 1978 (David Gower's first). I am sure he thought there would be headlines about Wasim Bari's complaint the next day. I have to say I could not believe any serious breach of the laws, or indeed the spirit of the laws, had escaped the scrutiny of umpires of the calibre of Dickie and Ken Palmer. As it turned out, both had warned the offenders and there was no cause for Bird, that conscientious perfectionist, to sleep uneasily on the hard board he has under his mattress to combat a longstanding back problem. But umpiring *is* a worrying job and on reflection I should have left him to enjoy his meal in peace.

That was the Test when Bob Willis, frustrated by England's failure to dismiss the Pakistan night-watchman Qasim, bowled a succession of bouncers at him before hitting him in the face and forcing him to leave the field. The umpires were under attack for not curbing Willis but his skipper Mike Brearley pointed out that Qasim was a batsman who had played long innings in his career and was not the normal tailender.

Back in 1949 I had the task of hunting out Dickie's Olympian predecessor Frank Chester to break the news that under the rules at the time, he had allowed England to make an illegal declaration on the Saturday evening of the Lord's Test against New Zealand. Chester, who was regarded as well nigh infallible with his brilliant decisions and mastery of the laws, had slipped up. The fact that no-one had noticed it was no consolation. I had ruined his Sunday lunch.

Walter Hadlee, the New Zealand captain, let him off the hook by laughing the matter off. Walter, father of Richard and the other cricketing Hadlees, set an example of sportsmanship later by chasing after Cyril Washbrook after he was the victim of a dodgy lbw and escorting him back to the crease. What a shame such a gesture failed to set standards ever since.

Chester would be aghast at what Bird and his colleagues have to put up with from cheating appeals, repeated TV showings of controversial decisions and the antics of hyped-up players. I wonder how many other jobs outside sport could stand up to equally searching examinations?

Dickie's finest hour of many must have been shared with Tommy Spencer, one of our outstanding postwar umpires along with Syd Buller, Charlie Elliott and David Shepherd. It came in the 1975 World Cup Final between England and Australia and was a classic of skill, experience and endurance. Arriving at eight-thirty for the pre-match briefing, they stood from 11 a.m. to 8.43 p.m. while 118.4 overs were bowled, 18 wickets fell, including 5 Australian run-outs and a pitch invasion took place. And there wasn't a single gripe about their performance from a player or spectator. And all for £100 each!

Money was never Dickie's motivation. He proved that by spurning an offer from Kerry Packer to join his World Series Cricket in Australia. The source of his success has always been his honest passion for cricket. With his trademark Norman Wisdom type white hat, his famous back-peddling sprint to get into position for run-outs, he has become a national sporting treasure. His sheer enthusiasm makes him a natural character for television. Indeed nobody gives the bird to Dickie but his popularity should never disguise the fact that he is an umpire among the greats of his difficult profession. That is his deserved place.

John Helm
Freelance television commentator and
President of Baildon CC

———

Recalls an incidental meeting Dickie had with Pavarotti.

There are probably more stories about Dickie than anyone else in the game. One I like was about the time he had a very long, tiring day at one of the Essex grounds. Someone told me he had stood out there in boiling heat for 120 overs and when play finally ended at eight forty-five he was so bleary-eyed that he walked straight off the pitch and towards a nearby lake. If someone hadn't grabbed him, he might have gone straight into it!

He tells me this one is true but a few years ago he was swimming off a beach in Barbados when he collided with a rather huge man. Dickie always introduces himself to people when he meets them for the first time and he said, 'Good morning sir, I'm Dickie Bird the Test match umpire.' The man was slightly bemused. 'I'm Pavarotti,' he said.

I was present the day Dickie scored his 181. The lights were on in the committee room and the selectors were picking the team for the next match. When Brian Sellers told him he had been dropped it must have been one of the biggest let-downs any sportsman could have experienced. But as one door closed ... another opened for Dickie and what a success he's made of it!

Bill Tidy

Helen Bertodano
The *Sunday Telegraph*

___

Helen visits Dickie's home ... a shrine to his career.

You would be forgiven for thinking that a man who fills his front room with over 100 photographs, portraits, cartoons – even a tapestry – of himself must be arrogant. Not Dickie Bird. To meet the world's most famous umpire is to understand the difference between arrogance and pride.

For Dickie Bird's predominant emotion is one of gratitude. He can scarcely believe that the game has done so much for him. In return he has turned his Yorkshire house – and indeed his whole life – into a shrine to cricket. 'I've given everything to cricket. I've never married. I'm married to cricket, you see.'

I can hardly fail to see. Even the safety grille inside the front door is forged out of iron bars cast in the shape of interlocking golden cricket bats. Signed bats are propped against the wall, a glass cabinet is filled with cricket balls and trophies and Dennis Lillee's tie hangs in the corner. A framed card inviting Mr Harold Bird to lunch with the Queen is on the mantelpiece, next to the menu detailing his meal with John Major at Chequers – quail's eggs followed by roast venison.

Yet despite the innumerable accolades, he is constantly seeking reassurance, particularly now that he has just made the hardest decision of his life. Although he is only sixty-two and does not have to retire until 1998, he has chosen to leave international cricket this summer, and the shockwaves are still reverberating through his psyche.

'Do you think I've done the right thing?' he asks me, of all people. 'I wanted to go out at the right time and be remembered with dignity. I didn't want people to say Dickie Bird was slipping.'

The phone rings for the first of many times during the morning and an almost identical conversation takes place. 'Do you think I did the right thing?' he asks the caller.

Speaking to his sister, Marjorie Wyatt, later that day, I

realize it is more than a conversational tic. 'It drives me mad,' she says with fondness. 'He's been asking me all week what I think about him going, and to be honest, it shocked me, yet he never mentioned it before he made up his mind. At the end of the day, he always knows what is best and does exactly what he thinks anyway.'

But decisions, at least those that are taken off the field, do not come easily to Dickie. Even a simple arrangement, like where we are going to sit, becomes semi-farcical. 'Shall we sit here or there?' he asks, pointing to two rooms either side of the front door. 'Whichever suits you,' I reply.

'Well, let's sit here then,' he suggests doubtfully, leading the way into the main sitting room. But he looks unhappy. 'It's entirely up to you, but we could move through here,' he says, diving towards the kitchen-cum-study next door. 'OK,' I say, following him. He starts pulling a chair over to the desk, strewn with letters and offers from publishers. 'I usually sit through here though,' he says, looking towards the sitting room. To cut a long story short, we end up in the sitting room.

He explains happily that he worries about everything. He nearly didn't go to umpire in India recently because he was worried about the pneumonic plague. 'And if there is nothing to worry about, I invent something.'

Every time he leaves the house, he invariably returns to check something. 'I'll be charging down the motorway and I'll suddenly wonder if I've turned the gas fire off. So I come back, and when I leave again I worry whether I remembered to turn the burglar alarm back on.'

To forestall all these potential crises, he always makes sure he has several hours in hand. For lunch at Buckingham Palace he left his seventeenth-century cottage in the mining village of Staincross, near Barnsley, at 5.30 a.m. and arrived at the Palace gates three hours later. 'The police recognized me and said, "You're a bit early for lunch, we haven't had the Changing of the Guard yet." So I went and sat in a coffee shop around the corner for four hours.'

The event itself was one of the happiest days of his life. He was particularly worried about the grapes, which he decided to avoid as he knew they had to be cut with scissors. Yet when the moment came, he thought it would be rude to refuse. 'They all went over the floor but the Queen said, "Don't worry, Dickie, the corgis will look after them." She made me feel so comfortable.'

The Prime Minister was more accommodating when he arrived early. He tells these stories in a tone of surprise, as if a force beyond control lands him at the appointed place well before the appointed hour. 'I was supposed to be at Chequers at twelve o'clock and somehow got there at nine-thirty so the police rang John Major and he said, 'If it's Dickie send him through.' So I went and sat with John and Norma for two and a half hours, nattering about cricket.' Didn't John Major have to run the country that morning, I ask? 'Oh no,' exclaims Dickie. 'It was a Sunday, you see.'

'He's always been a bag of nerves,' says Martyn Moxon, the former Yorkshire captain. 'Before a match, he stalks around, rabbiting on and on. I think it gives him the nervous energy he needs to go out there.'

Once on the pitch, he shows a swift and unerring judgement. Wearing his distinctive white cap, he twitches incessantly, hops around in agitation and stares maniacally at his light meter. But he has an extraordinary instinct for the right verdict. It is only in the past year or so that a couple of his decisions have been called into question, and a fear of ruining his reputation with a serious error has perhaps influenced his decision to depart.

'I don't think anyone in his sixties can be as good as when he is in his forties,' he says, sadly. He has had a good innings. In twenty-three years he has umpired 65 Tests, 92 one-day internationals and 3 World Cup finals. 'No-one in history has done that,' he states proudly. Dickie repeats this a couple of times. 'If I say something, nine times out of ten I will repeat myself,' he says, repeating even this without a hint of irony.

Bird may be eccentric but he is no idiot. Although the cricketers play practical jokes on him, they have the greatest respect for him. His countenance can quickly change to one of thunderous scorn if he disapproves of someone's behaviour.

Although technological advances have changed his job

drastically, Bird does not think the human umpire will ever be redundant. 'We need electronic aids for the close run-outs and close stumpings but that is all. I think umpires will be here until the end of time.'

Not this umpire, however. Although he will continue with county cricket for two years, 24 June will be his last day at international level, and he cannot contemplate that day at Lord's without great emotion. He speaks ponderously as though reciting a poem, 'When I walk down those stairs at Lord's through the Long Room at Lord's, when I walk down those stairs for the very last time, I think there will be a few tears shed.' He sighs deeply and shakes his head, 'Oh dear! I've got a tear in my eye even now.'

He invests it with such great drama that you have to pinch yourself to remember that this is not a life and death situation. But to Dickie, of course, it is everything, and it must have taken a great deal of courage to make his decision. 'He has nothing outside cricket,' says his sister Marjorie, who lives nearby and cleans for him. 'He's like a recluse in Barnsley.'

Although close to marriage on three occasions, he never went ahead. 'I have lived my life out of a suitcase and I know I could not be fair to a wife.' Dressed in torn slippers and an old sweatshirt, he has an engaging smile which lights up his face. He is an emotional man and is usually poised between chuckles and tears. Sometimes the two combine. 'I've cried for joy on occasion,' he says earnestly.

One of his biggest regrets is not having a son in whom he can inspire the same devotion to cricket. Coming from a close-knit family, he speaks lovingly of his parents, particularly his mother, with whom he lived until her death. 'You can have all the friends in the world, but your mother is your best friend. She will never let you down.'

Harold Bird, who was nicknamed Dickie at school, wishes his father could have witnessed his success. A miner, he never wanted Dickie to follow him into the pits and encouraged him as a cricketer. As Majorie says, 'Cricket domineered – and I mean domineered – the household when we were children.'

Dickie hopes that he will be able to act as a referee now and travel the world watching Test matches. He has even received an invitation from Paul Getty to become resident umpire on his own cricket pitch. Although umpiring is not particularly lucrative, he says that he is 'comfortable' financially. 'What worries me is that if I sit here where you see me now' – he pats the side of his tall crimson armchair – 'I will just worry myself away. I'd be dead within twelve months.'

A deeply religious man, Bird prays at his bedside every morning and night and says he will take in his stride whatever the future holds for him. 'I am prepared to suffer now because I am so grateful to the good Lord for everything he has given me, particularly my MBE, which means more to me than my own life.'

Ray Illingworth, paying tribute to Dickie Bird, says that besides being the greatest umpire in history, he has no malice. Bird agrees vigorously, saying he has never disliked or criticized anyone. But, rather than basking in self-glorification, he worries that it might mask a failing. 'I'm the type of bloke that never questions anything. Probably I don't fight for the things I should fight for.'

In a rare moment of self-analysis, he adds that his docility is partly due to shyness. 'If aunties and uncles came to visit us when I was a child, I would always go out of the room. I was probably shy with girls, too.' He repeats this last sentence three times.

He admits to loneliness but says he has become too set in his ways ever to share his life now. One suspects that he prefers his solitude and uses cricket as an excuse, a shield against intrusion.

'I only ever think about cricket,' he explains. 'In the middle of the night I jump up, dreaming that bowlers are appearing at me, shouting, "Howzat! Howzat!"'

Won't it be nice to watch cricket matches in the future without worrying about hairline decisions? 'No,' he says bluntly, 'I'll miss it.' The words are invested with such gruff emotion that for once he does not feel the need to repeat himself.

Reproduced with permission from the Sunday Telegraph.

Simon Hughes
Former Middlesex and Durham bowler, now a
sportswriter for the *Daily Telegraph*

'Yozzer' tells of the day he went to the jacuzzi with Dickie.

He's predominantly a lonely man, Dickie Bird. You don't need
to see him dining on his own in Bryan's fish restaurant near
Headingley, or watch him fuss over some minor detail on the
pitch or notice he's missed a few bristles with the razor to realize there's no-one for him to come home to or confide in. The
game is his wife.

He needs to talk. Any time. Any place. He turns up to
Yorkshire pre-season nets, crouching over the stumps,
exchanging chit-chat with the bowlers. 'What are you doing,
Dickie?' 'Joost gettin' me eye in.' He gabbles with the fielders
all the way out to the middle and all the way back.

'Someone find a boos to get Cowans back to his mark, else
we'll be 'ere all night,' he says to Mike Gatting at midwicket.
'OVER, LEFT HAND,' he shouts at the end of one, just in case
people had forgotten for a moment. The only reason he says
'Not art' so often is because you don't actually get to say anything if you send a batsman on his way.

Twice he stopped me in mid-run-up. I was ploughing in
against the wind once at Headingley when suddenly he stuck
out his left arm. 'Eee that man Boycott's joost arrived on
t'pavilion balcony,' he said, completely out of the blue. 'Look at
'im, 'e's got millions but 'e keeps it all to 'imself you know.
When 'e dies, they'll bury the money with 'im. And I'll be the
first to go an' dig it oop!'

A year later heavy rain delayed the start of a Benson and
Hedges match at Southampton until after lunch. Dickie and I
took the chance to relax in the health club beside the pavilion, ambling between the sauna, steam room and then the
jacuzzi which he clearly hadn't experienced before. At first
he tried to get in wearing his long johns. Eventually he
stripped down to his war issue Y-fronts and almost dozed off

in the warm, frothy water.

A strong wind dried the ground and when play began, I was given the new ball and confronted by the Smith brothers, hungry for runs. I was quite nervous. Running in for my third delivery, Dickie's arm went out again, I assumed as there was debris blowing across the pitch or because he'd dropped one of the six miniature beer barrels he used as counters. I came to a stop beside him and he said, 'Eee it were grand in that booble bath, wannit?'

Running up to bowl has never been the same since. Nor has taking a jacuzzi.

Derek Pringle

Former Essex and England all rounder and now the
respected cricket correspondent of the *Independent*

---

*Fellow bachelor Pringle reveals why bowlers used to queue up at
the opposite end to where Dickie was standing.*

If the people at Disney ever feel the urge to create a cartoon
character from cricket, they need look no further than Test
umpire Harold Dennis 'Dickie' Bird. With his trademark flat
white hat and a whole repertoire of idiosyncratic tics and
twitches, he is more famous than all but a handful of Test
cricketers, proving that, for the chosen few, fame and vocation
can still find you after 40.

Mind you, the animators will have to hurry if they want to
catch him live in all his splendour. After donning said white
cap and coat for 66 Tests, 95 one-day internationals – including
three World Cup finals – and 27 years of hairline adjudication,
His Dickieness is about to hang them up, and retire from the
international arena.

He will be 64 next birthday and feels that younger umpires
ought to be given a chance in what he believes is an increasingly arduous but better paid job. Still umpiring well – he came
third last year on marks given by county captains – he decided
some time ago that next week's Test at Lord's would be his
last, though he plans to carry on at county level for another
season.

'It's going to be something special though,' said Bird, whose
pay package for his first Test in 1973 came to £25 – the current
fee is £2,200. 'There is nothing to compare with Lord's on Test
match day. And when I walk down the steps from the umpires'
room, down through the Long Room and out on to the grass,
it will be a very emotional occasion for me, and I think I'll
probably shed a few tears.'

Well, won't we all. It is a sad fact of this grim age of
standardization that characters who can combine a high level
of skill with the propensity for fun, are increasingly rare. Even

186

us bowlers, who have cursed and spat our disbelief at rejected lbws, will miss him, in spite of the constant stream of 'not outs' that have emanated over the years from this hardest of umpires to impress when pads are struck.

In fact, Dickie's mere presence in a county match seems to bring on a bout of irrational behaviour among seam bowlers. After a career of trying to connive and jostle for the downhill, wind-assisted end, they are suddenly happy to take on gales and Eiger-like slopes just to be away from him in the belief that any inquiries for lbws are far more likely to be answered in the affirmative by the other umpire.

'People say I'm a "not outer". Well I probably have been hard on lbws. But one thing I've always tried to be is consistent to both teams. In any case, I was involved in a Test out in Port of Spain, between the West Indies and Pakistan, where there were 17 lbws in the match. That's a world record, though, of course, I didn't give them all,' he smirked, with a knowing glint of a man unlikely to go out in a blaze of leg-befores.

The fledgling Bird, who went to the local secondary modern in Barnsley, and played a lot of football as well as cricket, was far less cautious, he assures you. 'My big mate was Tommy Taylor, who died in the Munich air disaster. I played inside-right with him at school and did well enough to be approached by Sheffield Wednesday and one or two other First Division clubs.'

However, nothing came of football, so he played cricket for Yorkshire instead, joining them in 1956 when they closely shadowed Surrey as the most dominant county force in the land.

As an opening batsman, he admits to being something of a struggler and a regular berth for his native county eluded him. Undeterred, he left and joined Leicestershire in 1959. The move was prompted when he was dropped following an unbeaten 181 against Glamorgan – his highest first-class score – on a raging turner at Bradford Park Avenue.

'There was a selection committee of 39 there that game, and I remember Brian Sellers coming into the dressing-room and saying: "Well played Birdy, but get thee head down, thar's in second team next match. We've dropped thee." Mind you, I wouldn't have minded so much if it had been a flat pitch.'

He retired in 1964, but did not apply to become an umpire until 1969. A spell of coaching at Plymouth College sustained him until J. J. Warr, the former Middlesex and England fast bowler, suggested he apply for the umpires' list.

'At the time I thought "you must be joking. Umpiring, that's the worst job in the world." But I gave it some thought and when some of me old mates at Yorkshire reckoned it were probably the next best thing to playing, I applied.

'My first game was Yorkshire *v* Surrey at the Oval in 1970. I was so nervous I arrived at a quarter to six in the morning, so as not to be late. Of course the gates were shut, so I had some explaining to do when a London Bobby caught me trying to climb in.'

It is not the only time he has been the early bird: he arrived four hours early at Buckingham Palace to have lunch with the Queen and receive an MBE – an event, he says, that was the best day of his life.

Keith Fletcher, Essex's Godfather and guru, reckons Bird is easily the best and most consistent Test umpire he's seen and tougher than he makes out. The impression of being frail and downtrodden with worry is simply a mask.

Certainly, he has never run away from the issue of intimidatory bowling. Many will remember the blazing rows over excessive use of the bouncer with Clive Lloyd at Edgbaston in 1984 and Andy Roberts, when he was coaching the West Indies at Old Trafford last year. But in this controversial area that continues to blight the game, he has never once been publicly backed by the Test and County Cricket Board.

Apart from two holidays a year at the Livermead Cliff hotel, where he likes to breakfast every morning on kippers, he relaxes, he claims, by worrying. He doesn't mind criticism, and as long as people get their facts right he accepts it as part of the traditional banter that goes on in the pub afterwards.

'With all the money coming into the game, the need for the perfect decision is growing, though I don't like the mass appealing that has crept in with it. There is no doubt that the use of electronic aids for line decisions has been a tremendous help. I can see it being used soon for low catches [like Graeme

Hick's scooped catch at slip to dismiss Vikram Rathore at Edgbaston] but not for other decisions.'

He has seen more of the modern greats from closer quarters than most, rating Dennis Lillee's 5 for 15 and John Edrich's 37 on a treacherous rain-affected pitch at Edgbaston in 1975 as the best bowling and batting he's seen. Surprising then, that he does not mourn the demise of uncovered pitches.

Nor, he claims, will he miss the briefcase full of formulas and conversion charts that now accompanies the modern umpire.

'When I started I thought umpiring was giving them in, or giving them out. All that's changed and although after Lord's I'll miss the buzz of the Test matches, I'll not miss those bloomin' maths tables.'

Alan Fraser
Sports Feature writer, *Daily Mail*

———

Scotsman Alan, who does not claim to be a cricket expert, spends a convivial hour with Dickie at Fenner's.

Everybody loves the old chap but, mark my words, by next weekend people will be flying to the furthest corners of the world not to avoid Euro 96 but because they cannot bear to hear another Dickie Bird anecdote.

So here's one now. 'A tremendous character, Mervyn Hughes,' Bird said. 'I remember when Australia were here last. He was bowling from my end to Graeme Hick and he was swearing at Mr Hick.

'I said "Look here, Mervyn, I don't want you to swear at this man. He has done you no harm. Why are you swearing?" I said: "I want you to get on with your bowling and I want you to be a good lad, Mervyn."

'He walked past me to bowl next ball and he looked at me and his moustache were quivering and he said: "Dickie Bird," he said, "you're a legend".'

Hughes was, of course, dead right. Only a legend could command the kind of global media coverage 63-year-old Bird is attracting as he prepares to umpire his 66th and final Test match this week, the Lord's meeting between England and India.

Interviews with Radio 1, 2, 4 and Five Live, a special profile to be broadcast on BBC television tomorrow night – with tribute by Prime Minister John Major – a press conference tomorrow afternoon organized by the Test and County Cricket Board, an item on ITV's *News at Ten* and countless features in broadsheets and tabloids alike, here and abroad. And all without even a fingernail of public relations manipulation from Max Clifford.

Two books are being published with an official autobiography to follow at Christmas 1997. There were also recent appearances on *Desert Island Discs* and *Breakfast With Frost*, no less. Most of them will have been told the Merv tale – and half a dozen of his classic stories – and all will be fully aware of the emotions surrounding his Lord's farewell.

'When I walk down those steps from the Umpires Room, through the Long Room with all the members sitting in their high chairs, and on to the green, I shall have a few tears in my eyes. I'm not afraid to admit it. Oh, I will that.'

Who would doubt it? Tears stopped play – or at least delayed – would be entirely appropriate for the man who was credited with ending a five-year drought in Sharjah and with opening the previously locked heavens in Bulawayo merely by being there in an umpiring capacity.

'As soon as I walked off the plane in Zimbabwe a spot of rain hit me on the head,' he recalled. A spot of embellishment more like, but this goes with the territory and our affection for Bird is in no way diminished by the knowledge that truth and fiction sometimes blur and that – probably without intent – he encourages the mythology surrounding this quintessential English eccentric.

There is, of course, his obsessive fear of being late. So much so that he has arrived hours early for drinks at Downing Street, lunch at Chequers and his investiture at Buckingham Palace. There was, too, his legendary dawn raid on the Oval gates prior to his very first county championship match, Surrey *v* Yorkshire, in May, 1970.

'Oh aye, always early,' he said as we sat in the pavilion at Fenner's last Friday. 'I were here at 8.30 this morning.' The Cambridge University gateman had clocked him at 9.10 but let's not quibble about 40 minutes. By 9.30 he was doing his first telephone interview of the day.

'Cricket is my hobby,' he was heard to say. 'I think about only cricket in my spare time.' There were to be four telephone interruptions during our chat, 'Dickie, telephone,' the tea lady would shout as if she had been doing it for the past quarter of a century. Which she has. She and dozens like her around the county grounds of England.

It had been a typical week for Dickie. A one-day match on Sunday, a second XI fixture at Northampton for the first part of the week and now the start of three days at Fenner's for

Cambridge University *v* Hampshire. He was in a right state. He is always in a right state. 'What time is it? Oh dear.'

Play was not due to start for 75 minutes and there was not a cloud in the sky but Dickie, as ever, was anxious. 'I'm a bit highly strung,' he said. 'Have you got enough, mate? Oh, come on, mate. I've got things to do. I haven't even had a cup of tea yet.'

It was not immediately apparent what in umpiring terms there was to do but he's the boss. 'Is it marked out yet?' he enquired about the pitch of no-one in particular. 'Better have a look, see what's doing.' he ventured to his fellow umpire Martin Reid, who reacted with an affectionate, if slightly indulgent, smile. Then a wonderful thing happened. Start of play was still an hour off when the Queen Mother of English cricket walked down the pavilion steps to be greeted with the shout 'Dickie' from a group of players doing stretching exercises on the grass.

In that single 'Dickie' you could sense a touch of mockery, dollops of warmth and oodles of respect. As Dickie says – and he will say time and again this week: 'Money can't buy that. Respect means more to me than all the money in the world.'

One by one, the older hands of Hampshire came to shake his hand and pay their respects. Not just the batsmen, though long ago he acquired the reputation of being a 'not out' umpire.

'I wouldn't say I have been that,' he said. 'I would say this. I have been a consistent umpire. That's one of the most important things in umpiring. That's all the players ask for.'

The truth is that, for all his mannerisms and idiosyncrasies and for the minor disasters and comical episodes which have accompanied his time in the middle, he would never have become the most instantly recognizable figure in English cricket had he not been a damn fine umpire.

Just how this shambling, nervous, indecisive person in civvies became the umpiring equivalent of Superman when donning a white coat and white flat cap remains a mystery. 'I suppose I just stumbled into the thing I was meant to do,' he suggested. We had reached the square at Fenner's.

'Is there a rope round?' he asked, wondering if the boundary had been clearly defined. He reacted to news that a couple of trees might be overhanging the boundary as one would to the death of a relative.

'Looks like a lot of runs in that,' I ventured by way of conversation as we gazed at the wicket. 'I haven't a clue, mate. I don't know anything about wickets. What do you think?' he replied.

Bliss. To be asked about a track by Dickie Bird. 'Might take turn,' I suggested sheepishly.

Pretty soon, Dickie could be seen in familiar pose. Slightly hunched, he peered down that 22 yards, occasionally skipping arthritically out of the way of the ball magnetically drawn to his lower limbs, scampering sideways like a crab to judge a possible run out, wiping his worried brow, looking anxiously at the clear blue skies.

Time, perhaps, to reflect on all that he has seen. Best bowler – Dennis Lillee; best batsman – Barry Richards, he thought; best all-rounder – Sir Garfield Sobers; most exciting match – Pakistan *v* Australia in Karachi last year.

He might even have rehearsed an anecdote or two. For example, England *v* West Indies. 'We were all walking up to the members' enclosure at Old Trafford and there were a Lancashire member shouting and bawling at me. "What have you brought them off for this time? Is it bad light?" I said "No, sir, it's lunchtime".'

For Harold 'Dickie' Bird, Test umpire extraordinaire, it's nearly stumps.

9

SON OF BARNSLEY

Dickie, a confirmed bachelor, leads a simple life. A regular churchgoer, he is a man whose life follows a regular pattern.

Lord Mason of Barnsley

Formerly Roy Mason, MP, Lord Mason is a former Minister for Northern Ireland. He is one of Dickie's oldest friends.

Most Sundays when he is not away umpiring, Dickie, my wife and I and a few friends will meet for a lunchtime drink. There is Ashley Jackson, the Yorkshire watercolour artist, Stan Richards, the actor who plays Seph in *Emmerdale,* and one or two others. Dickie has one subject, and one subject only, to talk about and that is cricket. He is not the slightest bit interested in politics.

He is instantly recognizable wherever he goes and although it can be a little disruptive to be accosted by strangers when you are sitting talking to friends I have never known him be rude to anyone. Nor have I heard him pass a rude word about anyone. He is as honest as the day is long and I am absolutely convinced that his achievements in the field of umpiring will never be equalled, certainly not bettered.

There is too much pressure on umpires today. Maybe

Dickie survived it better than anyone because he is a born worrier and had so much experience worrying that he was well trained to handle the pressure when it came! He will wake in the middle of the night and find something to worry about.

They say of some famous people that they will rise too high and forget their roots and the people they knew on the way up. No-one could ever say that of Dickie. Born and bred in Barnsley, as I was, he still lives there. I first met him when he was a Colt with Yorkshire. I had been down the mines myself for fourteen years but didn't know his father who was a miner all his life.

Dickie is a regular at Madge's Café in Wellington Street, Barnsley. It is in a little side-street and seats about twenty people. His favourite dish is Irish stew and dumplings. He once mentioned it during a radio interview and business boomed for a while afterwards.

Dickie is a creature of habit, a fitness fanatic. He religiously exercises for up to half an hour in the bathroom every morning and will not be disturbed. Like a lot of people who basically enjoy a fairly lonely life, he loves walking. He will walk miles when he is not working. I know because my wife and I will go on long walks with him when we are on holiday at the same time in his favourite resort of Torquay.

His house on the outskirts of Barnsley is a fortress. It has to be because everyone knows when he is away and the house is unattended. There are steel bars protecting the windows and a steel shutter backing onto the front door. Once he had to call out the fire brigade because he was unable to unlock the steel shutter on the door! Firemen put their ladders up outside and had to climb in through an upstairs window. I joked that he would have to pay the bill.

I believe he is the only man who stopped a Test match in this country because he needed to go to the toilet. It was a match at Old Trafford and he suddenly announced to the players, 'Gentlemen, nature calls.' It must have mystified the crowd and the commentators but those in the pavilion must have had a clue when he emerged down the pavilion steps zipping himself up.

He has been an outstanding ambassador on behalf of our country and has gained the respect of the whole cricketing world.

Dean Chester
Manager of Bryan Ellison, chemists, Barnsley

———

A former footballer with Sheffield Wednesday, Dean Chester takes a keen, personal interest in Dickie's medical needs.

Dickie is one of our regular customers. His doctor's surgery is across the road and he will come in with a prescription. He travels abroad so much that he will often be in to check what he needs to take for the various parts of the world he is travelling to. I don't know of anyone who takes their obligations so seriously. He does everything he can to ensure he doesn't go down with something and can't do his job properly.

I remember one day he cost me a day off. I was rung up and asked to come in to give him advice. I've never held it against him. As far as I know, he's never picked up an illness abroad. When he goes to India and Pakistan he will take plenty of bottled water and chocolate to keep him going.

He used to take garlic tablets regularly and now he takes cod-liver oil tablets, the real big ones. He was at a do with Sir Stan Matthews once and Stan told him he took Biostrath every day. Dickie said, 'If it's good enough for him, it's good enough for me. I'd like to live as long as he has.'

Dickie also gargles with Listerine every day and he does his back exercises on his bathroom floor every morning. He's very fit for his age.

Stewart Blackburn
Manager, Madge's Café

Stewart runs Madge's Café in Wellington Street, Barnsley. It seats twenty-four customers and Dickie is often one of them.

When he is in the country, Dickie pops in several times a week for his lunch. His favourite is stew and dumplings at £1.25. He used to have baked beans on toast or Yorkshire pudding.

He comes in on his own – I don't think he does any cooking at home – but everyone knows him and they'll all be talking to him and having a laugh and a joke. My wife pulls his leg all the time. He's on telly more often than most famous people and he will tell us about things that went on in games.

He's the most famous person who comes in. We have had a few actors from the theatre down the road as well I suppose. My mother used to run the café and he's been coming here as long as I can remember. We take him for what he is, an ordinary bloke from Barnsley.

Jim Gratton
Owner of Brooklands Restaurant and Motel in Barnsley

Jim Gratton has known Dickie more than twenty years and knows all his food fads.

Dickie comes in most Sundays for his Sunday lunch – usually fish or maybe roast beef with Yorkshire pudding. He's not a big eater but we do give the customers big portions. Fred Trueman once said, 'It's fair troughing here, lad!'

Occasionally when he is hungry he will have a Barnsley chop. He'll come in on his own but everyone talks to him and I always marvel at his patience with boys. He will answer all their questions and give them advice about their cricket, sign autographs and all that kind of thing.

My wife Georgetta is Italian and doesn't understand cricket but she loves to see his mannerisms when a Test match is on and he is appearing. You can't mistake the way he stands.

Dickie isn't much of a drinker. He'll have a glass of red wine or a half of beer. He tends to drink red wine now after his doctor told him it's good for his circulation.

He's been coming here ever since I took over the place but I'm sixty-five and I've sold out to a developer who wants to build a supermarket. In eighteen months time I'll be leaving and I don't think the locals will forgive me. I don't know what Dickie will do.

Cricket is a way of life to him. Money isn't important to him: he just loves the game and talking about it.

Lord Howell of Aston
Former Sports Minister in the last Labour Government and ex-Football League referee

---

Lord Howell has a number of things in common with Dickie.
They have both officiated in top sport and share a love of holi-
daying in Devon and going on long walks.

Dickie has been a great friend of ours now for many years. We
stay at the same hotel in Torquay, the Livermead Cliff Hotel
where he goes to relax every year. I take a Church group of
about twenty people there and he entertains them with his
stories. He puts on a performance for them, free of charge.
They love him. We take him on our trips and wherever we go,
however small the village in Devon, people always recognize
him and come up to talk to him. He thrives on it.

Dickie belongs to a small Methodist Church in Barnsley
and when he is with us he attends a church in Torquay which
has a much larger congregation. One day he was examining
the notice they hand round to the congregation and saw that
the collection the previous week had come to £945. 'Crikey!'
he said. 'We're lucky if we get £9 in our church. They must be
a rich lot here!'

Dickie is someone who has great respect for people. When
we are having dinner he will tell a story and he'll suddenly say
'and y'know Lord Howell ...' I keep telling him the only title
you should have is the name you are christened with. He
normally calls me Denis but sometimes he gets carried away.

We have always agreed on one thing: the introduction of the
television camera to make decisions in both cricket and football is not a good thing because it undermines the authority of
the officials. And something that only applies at the top of the
sport and not throughout the sport surely cannot be right.

After one Test against Australia, he described a run-out
decision he made and said, 'And I told him, you're out lad, and
I'm not going to consult that damn fool of a camera in the
pavilion. It's down to me. You're out!'

He has been the one Test umpire who has regularly taken a stand against the overuse of short-pitched fast bowling. He's warned more bowlers than the others put together. After the last West Indies tour, he told me, 'I stopped 'em! Did you see me talking to Courtney Walsh? I stopped him!' He has a great sense of fairness and had the courage to act when it was necessary.

During the last series against Pakistan I remember a senior cricket official telling me that it had been a fraught series, with plenty of controversy and the Pakistan manager had told him, 'If Dickie had umpired all our matches there would not have been any trouble.'

When I was Sports Minister I asked the Treasury Solicitor if he cared to make a ruling on where the liability would lie if, God forbid, a batsman had been killed by a delivery from a bowler who had broken the spirit of the game by bowling too many short-pitched balls. The verdict was that as the batsman had willingly gone out to face that kind of bowling it was up to him. I have discussed this many times with Dickie and we both agree that if Law 42.8 was broken and no action had been taken by the umpires it would make an interesting test case.

I am glad he is retiring from the international scene when he is still at the top of the tree because as I have told him many times 'the moment to go is when they still want to see more of you.' It is a most exhausting job and I am glad he has taken my advice. I hope the authorities ensure he stays in the game in some capacity. He could give great service to the game talking to youngsters and aspiring umpires.

I have tremendous admiration for him: his enthusiasm is heart-warming and it is a joy to spend a few days with him every year.

10

POSTSCRIPT FROM TORQUAY

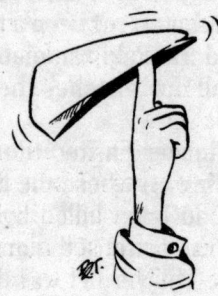

John Perry

John and his wife Pat run the Livermead Cliff Hotel in Torquay where Dickie goes to unwind every year. Dickie has been going there for more than twenty years.

Dickie is a man of habit. When he comes to us, about two or three times a year, he plans his route so that he stops at the same two Little Chefs for something to eat. He always has the same room, overlooking the sea and we have to provide a bed board because of his back.

When he arrives, he will leave his car in the car park and not use it again until he goes. He loves walking, up to five or six miles at a time. The bobble hat he wears out of season is well known around here. When it is warmer, he loves sitting on the promontory listening to Barbara Streisand tapes on his Walkman and reading a newspaper.

Everyone knows him in this area and he talks to them all, whether they are the King or a dustman. And he is immensely friendly to the staff who love him, as we all do. He is a dear man – an honest, simple man with simple tastes who is as straight as a gun barrel.

He is a very emotional man and when he comes down at the end of the cricket season he is shattered and we help him unwind. Years ago he would run along the beach every day but as you get older the legs tire and these days he confines his exercise to walking.

For breakfast he will insist on his usual haddock or kippers and we have to get in special supplies for him. His tea has to be served at the exact time in his meal. At lunch and dinner we have to prepare his special gravy.

He dines with Pat and myself in the evening and lately has taken to drinking a couple of glasses of red wine because his doctor says it is good for him. He won't touch white, or gin and tonic, or anything else. You will not see him go within a million miles of a night-club. He will be off to bed at ten-thirty, or eleven at the latest.

He was here when he announced he was retiring. He told me the news quite calmly but the next day, when the switchboard here wasn't up to taking all the media calls, he got into quite a state.

He worries about his health and his worry at the moment is his sinuses. He abhors smoking and if someone in the room is smoking you can see him inch away. On Sundays he walks to Cockington Church and is back for Sunday lunch. He loves puddings – cakes and chocolate sauce and all the extras.

The old ladies love him and the way he regales them with stories. He is so open and frank and has this wonderful ability to turn an ordinary occasion into a joyous one with his fun and laughter.

But essentially he is a private man and we respect that. I hope the roof comes off at Lord's when he walks out for the last time. He deserves that sort of acclaim for what he has done for cricket, the game he loves so much.

SUMMERS WILL NEVER BE THE SAME
A Tribute to Brian Johnston
Edited by Christopher Martin-Jenkins & Pat Gibson

'I understand there are some men who do not like cricket, but I
would not like my daughter to marry one'
Brian Johnston

Brian Johnston, who died in January 1994, was one of the best
loved figures on radio. His unique broadcasting style won him a
special place in the hearts of listeners everywhere.

Although 'Johnners' became known as the voice of cricket, he
was also a national figure as the presenter of *Down Your Way*. His
many other broadcasting credits include presenting for television
the Queen's Coronation and the Boat Race.

Most of all, Johnners will be remembered for his schoolboy
humour. Specially revised and updated for the paperback edition,
this volume of tributes includes anecdotes and memoirs from
over sixty colleagues and friends – including John Major, Sir
Colin Cowdrey, Richie Benaud, John Paul Getty, Lord Whitelaw,
Tim Rice, Lord Carrington and Jonathan Agnew – as well as short
extracts from Johnners' own publications and transcripts of some
of his most famous broadcasts.

0 552 99631 9

BEATING THE FIELD
My Own Story
by Brian Lara with Brian Scovell

On 18 April 1994 at the St John's Recreation Ground in Antigua, Brian Lara scored 375 against England for the West Indies, smashing the Test record set in 1958 by Sir Gary Sobers. On 6 June of the same year, he scored an unbeaten 501 against Durham at Edgbaston, beating Hanif Mohammed's record of 499. In eight first-class innings, he scored seven centuries. He is now indisputably the world's number-one batsman.

Beating the Field is Brian Lara's own story of his record-breaking career so far, one in which he has already achieved more than most cricketers do in a lifetime. The second youngest of a family of eleven, Lara reveals the philosophy that has taken him from the back streets of a small village, Santa Cruz, in Trinidad, to the cricketing heights.

Critical of county cricket and many of its regulations, Lara writes frankly about the behind-the-scenes dramas at Warwickshire as he helped them to a record-breaking season unparalleled in English cricket. He also gives his trenchant opinions on some of cricket's recent controversies. *Beating the Field* provides a unique insight into the mind of the biggest name to emerge in cricket for many years, a man whose ambition, as he told his sister Agnes when he was eight, was 'to become the greatest cricketer there has ever been.'

0 552 14350 2

BOYCOTT: THE AUTOBIOGRAPHY
by Geoffrey Boycott

Captain of Yorkshire and England, yet discarded by both when still at his peak, Boycott has been at the top for over twenty years. As a boy growing up in a Yorkshire mining community, he played cricket in the back streets with a manhole cover as a wicket, displaying even then the gritty determination which drove him on to become one of the greatest run-getters in Test history. Such brilliance, together with his steely courage when facing the fastest and most terrifying bowlers in the world, has led many to feel that he is the greatest batsman of our time. Boycott talks frankly about his often fiery relationships with such great cricketers as Illingworth, Trueman and Close, and about his love-hate relationship with Yorkshire cricket. He discusses his key partnerships with team-mates such as Denness, Brearley and Botham. And he speaks here for the first time about why he chose to opt out of Test cricket for three years in the mid-1970s.

'An admirably honest insight into one of sport's most complex characters'
Daily Telegraph

'Marvellously good, full of passion and observation'
Guardian

'Misguided, mishandled, criticised and crucified – and only because he's different.'
Brian Clough

0 552 99318 2

AN EVENING WITH JOHNNERS

by Brian Johnston

Memories and anecdotes as told by the master raconteur himself
edited and introduced by Barry Johnston

In early 1993, at the age of eighty, Brian Johnston embarked on
his first ever concert tour, a one man show called *An Evening with
Johnners* which blended stories from his life and career with the
many, often awful, jokes, for which he was renowned. The show
was a sell-out and the two recordings which were made from it –
An Evening with Johnners and *An Hour with Johnners* – continue
to be bestselling audiotapes.

This book combines material from both shows in one volume and
through its pages Brian Johnston's skill and warmth as a master
raconteur shine through. He recalls his years at Eton and Oxford,
his war service with the Grenadier Guards and his fortuitous leap
into the BBC for whom he worked for nearly fifty years.

Those years at the BBC provided him with a fund of glorious
memories and anecdotes, the best of which he describes here in
his inimitable style. Some, such as the famous 'leg-over' incident
with co-commentator Jonathan Agnew, have gone down in broadcasting history; others are less well-known and will be discovered
for the first time by the reader; all, however are a joy to read and
savour and will provide his many fans with unique opportunity to
sit down and enjoy *An Evening with Johnners*.

0 552 14494 0

A SELECTED LIST OF RELATED TITLES AVAILABLE FROM CORGI AND PARTRIDGE PRESS

99318 2	BOYCOTT: THE AUTOBIOGRAPHY	Geoffrey Boycott	£6.99
25256 1	JACK CHARLTON: THE AUTOBIOGRAPHY	Jack Charlton	£16.99
14003 1	CLOUGH THE AUTOBIOGRAPHY	Brian Clough	£5.99
14373 1	CLOUGH AUTOBIOGRAPHY AUDIO	Brian Clough	£8.99*
25240 5	PREGNANT AND FIT (Hardback)	Sharron Davies & Julia Thorley	£12.99
13937 8	THE FIRST FIFTY – MUNRO-BAGGING WITHOUT A BEARD	Muriel Gray	£8.99
13966 1	ALAIN PROST: A BIOGRAPHY	Christopher Hilton	£5.99
13754 5	AYRTON SENNA: THE HARD EDGE OF GENIUS	Christopher Hilton	£6.99
25182 4	BEHIND THE SCENES IN MOTOR RACING (Hardback)	Anthony Howard	£14.99
25180 8	BEHIND THE SCENES IN HORSE RACING (Hardback)	Charlie Hurt	£14.99
14494 0	AN EVENING WITH JOHNNERS	Brian Johnston ed. Barry Johnston	£6.99
14350 2	BEATING THE FIELD	Brian Lara with Brian Scovell	£5.99
99631 9	SUMMERS WILL NEVER BE THE SAME	Christopher Martin-Jenkins & Pat Gibson	£5.99
14484 3	BRIAN MOORE AUTOBIOGRAPHY	Brian Moore & Stephen Jones	£6.99
14153 4	LESTER PIGGOTT AUTOBIOGRAPHY	Lester Piggott	£5.99
25230 8	STEVEN REDGRAVE'S COMPLETE BOOK OF ROWING (Hardback)	Steven Redgrave	£17.99
25196 4	COMPLETE BOOK OF MINI RUGBY (Hardback)	Don Rutherford	£14.99
25228 6	OUT OF BOUNDS (Hardback)	Lauren St John	£16.99
14443 6	LESTER PIGGOTT AUDIO	Lester Piggott	£8.99*
13939 4	SEVE: BIOGRAPHY OF SEVE BALLESTEROS	Lauren St John	£6.99
25224 3	THE OPEN CHAMPIONSHIP 95 (Hardback)	Tom Tyrell	£14.99